I love my World

MENTORING PLAY IN NATURE, FOR OUR SUSTAINABLE FUTURE

Bushcraft, Environmental Art,
Nature Awareness and Outdoor Play Activities for
Parents, Forest Scholl leaders, Teachers, Play Rangers,
Aunties and Uncles... In fact anyone with a love of our world who
spends time outdoors and enjoy sharing it with others.

by Chris Holland
Wholeland Press, Otterton, 2009

Cover design by samskara design
Rear cover background photo by Martin Champness

ISBN: 978-0-9561566-0-0

Published by Wholeland Press, Otterton, England

Thanksgiving

There is a lot to give thanks for. First, All My Relations, second, All My
relations, and third, All my Relations! No, seriously, I give thanks for
all those elders, seen and unseen, who have been guardians and
mentors of the various skills, activities, games and stories I share with
you in this book.

Specifically I would like to thank Dom for walking through many
formative doorways with me and for his unfaltering brotherly love;
Adam Rose for introducing me to the plant people; Mr Bodger, Andy
Letcher, Patrick Whitefield and Jon Cree for helping me know I am a
teacher; Thomas Schorr-Kon for his teachings, friendship and
introducing me to the teachings of Stalking Wolf, Tom Brown Jr and
Jon Young; To Chris Salisbury and all at WildWise; Richard Irvine for
fine words, suggestions and help with the editing; Many children past
and present at Otterton School; The British government for working
families tax credits. Dottie for the title, Mum, Jo and Angela Hanna for
reading through the manuscript, Lucy Archer for the curriculum links
and last, but not least Wizz, who helped shape this book and make it
possible by doing the lioness's share of looking after our children
while I sat at the Mac.

Claim your must have Free bonus resources!

To get your copy of the **PDF file that links all the activities in
the book to the National Curriculum ('09)** and a video of
Chris Holland re-telling The Coming of the Dreamcatcher story,
email your name and address to chris@wholeland.org.uk now!

Contents

Water droplets on Aquilegias

Introduction

I love my World is for anyone with an interest in bushcraft, camping and the great outdoors, who wants ideas on how to connect with nature at a deep and practical level. It's for forest school leaders, outdoor educators and play rangers who have done some training but want more activity ideas. It's for parents and carers who want things to do with their children when out in the garden or in the woods, but are not sure where to start. It's also for teachers who want to take their classes outdoors, into the school grounds and beyond, but are not sure what activities to do and how to link the activities to the National Curriculum.

Most importantly, this book is for Nature, in the hope that through doing some of the activities we humans will feel a bit more love and respect for the world around us.

To begin with, a little story from long ago:

One day, beside a rushing stream in the Welsh mountains, I was talking to an elder I had met on the trail about stories. I told him I was interested in finding stories, from all over the world, which would help humans living at this brief moment in the earth's story to remember we are all part of the same community, the same web of life that includes the rock, the plant and the animal kingdoms. We had only a few minutes together before our paths went in different directions. As a droplet of sparkling water splashed onto a mossy pillow beside the trail, he told me this very simple story:

"There was a time when the creator sent a great race of rainbow people to live on this earth. They were a tribe of human creator spirits; people of many different skin colours – some were shades of green, some of brown... After a time these people became hungry and cold because then the land was barren. Nothing grew, called out or flew. There was no shelter, no food. The tribe gathered in a big heap to keep warm. Then one of them said, 'I know! Lets all change into different forms, so we can nurture and feed each other'."

"So it was that the people became the different plants and animals: plants that climbed, sprawled, and rooted, animals that crept, jumped and flew. Some of the people lay down and became the hills and mountains. Some of the people who remained as humans shed tears of grief over the changes in their relatives, and where their tears fell, lakes and rivers formed. The tribe truly did nurture, shelter and feed each other. Since that day the walking people, live each moment knowing that the plants, animals and rocks are all related, and when the rainbows come they are reminded of all the races without whom they could not live, and they remember what a wonderful place it is we live on, this planet we call Earth."

As He and I went our separate ways I couldn't help but feel my own sadness that we industrialized humans, with TVs, central heating, shoes, tractors and cars, have forgotten that the plants and animals are our relatives. They all share the same make up of nutrients from the soil, water and sunlight. Everything that lives on this earth is a result of the interaction of the Sun's energy with the elements of the earth. We are all interconnected systems of energy flow. We are life on earth, and it's about time we all felt some kinship with the planet again.

This book

This book is about many things. First, it is about inspiring us all to go and play, outside, in natural surrounding - in some woods perhaps. If not in the woods, then near some woods, in a park or maybe in a tiny copse at the end of your street, and if not there, then in the tiniest of back gardens! What if you don't have a garden to play in? There are moors, coasts, rivers and hedgerow throughout this green and pleasant land waiting to be enriched with the sound of people at play.

Second, these pages are brimming with pictures from all kinds of habitats to remind us of the wonders of natural design, and also to help you see how the activities and crafts work.

Tansy flowers

I aim to take you and your students on a journey to feel the wholeness of community, in a planetary sense. I share a few little day trips and excursions along the way; first into yourself, to understand that **we are all one** on this planet. The basic survival skills that follow are there to help you feel at home, and self-reliant. From then on the path widens, and we visit the craftsman, the scribe, the artist and the map maker, the hunter and the caretaker, the healer and the bard, before tying the threads of the journey together and revisiting the community we came from, fresh, 're-wilded' and full of the joy of Nature.

I hope you will find this book a comfortable blend of philosophy, information and instruction, which will give a background understanding and context to the activities, thus bringing a depth to the experience of these for both the leader and the participants. The activities, games and crafts are a mixture of bushcraft, environmental art, nature awareness and story-making that help us directly experience the world we live in. They are suggestions, inspiration for you to find ways that suit your style of playing, mentoring or teaching. The whole book is a course in its own right: you can follow it step by step. You can also simply pick out an activity suited for the moment.

Disclaimer

Throughout this book I do my best to philosophically and practically prepare you to deliver the activities, so it is now up to you to try the activities out, put them to the test and refine them as you see fit. At all times you remain responsible for the way in which you deliver the activities, voice your opinions and manage your groups.

A family outing to Shapwick Nature Reserve, Somerset.

Fire making with The Women's Adventure Group, South Devon

About the activities

The activities are laid out in a **'ready, get set, go'** format, with an occasional follow on section **'useful things to know'**. When writing the book I felt it best to start at the basics and so you may feel a bit 'spoon fed' at times. The '**Ready**' section is to introduce the activity, to explain some of the reasons why to do it and prepare you mentally to lead the activity. '**Get set**' helps you get physically prepared. '**Go**' details how I lead the session. You can then lead it in your own way. The section '**Useful things to know**' (for the activity leader), offers relevant tips, facts and sometimes extension and activity ideas, to complement and run-on from the session.

I love my World is about listening. Listening to the world around us, to the subtle language of sound, to the language of the birds, the song of the grain in the piece of wood you are carving, to the telltale silencing of the crickets as someone creeps through the grass. It's about listening to our hearts, and to the call of the wild.

10

This book is also about telling stories. The activities within work in reconnecting people with nature. I share them with you, for the greater good of all. The land bristles with its own stories for the careful listener to hear and understand. There are many stories yet to be told, perhaps some of them inspired by activities in this book. Such stories breathe life into the spirit of the land. May we embrace the playful, joyous movement of spring, and the expectant, poised stillness in winter and feel a part of the ongoing story-cycle of the land.

Thanks to Uncle Marto for this beautiful late winter photo.

I hope that this book goes some way to helping you feel kinship with all our relations and experience the awesomeness and beauty of the natural world of which we are a part, in a playful, practical and timeless way. I hope that you may come to see this book as a tool, which, when used in conjunction with other teaching ideas, becomes part of your Education for Sustainability toolkit (if you have one or even want one, that is!).

Teaching with the flow

Everything in nature flows in cycles and spirals. Everything has its own time, place and direction, including a learning journey. Great teachings come from years of experience, often the accumulated experience of all the teachers, going way back, to our Ancestors. Equally, many great moments of understanding and wonder are crafted by inspired teachers, who in the moment, combine content with context. Teaching effectively outdoors requires a mixture of forward planning, being prepared, going with the flow, and being spontaneous.

One of the guidelines by which I try to live is "work with Nature, not against", so when it comes to teaching, I try to read the nature of the group I am working with, so I can teach effectively. I have noticed that each group has its own feeling or 'field', and within it is a mixture of needs from the individual students. 'Reading' the group and fine planning have sometimes to be done on the hoof, and occasionally the best-laid plans have to change. There are many challenges and huge rewards from working with children and Nature, even on a wet summer camp when it seems like it is never going to stop raining!

Learn to play, play to learn

Over the years, my teaching has been influenced by several teaching tools, technologies, principles and people that I would like to share with you now, before you set off on the journey of reading this book. I like to think of it as 'tipping out the tool bag', to share with you some of my favourite implements, gizmos and gadgets – the key ideas and attitudes that help me facilitate a "learn to play, play to learn" experience.

The tool bag itself is made is of a very special fabric woven from strong yarns of intention to create self-esteem, self-empowerment, and flecked with respect and love for all life forms.

Let's look at the tools within the bag. You may already be familiar with the concept of 'flow learning' put forward by Joseph Cornell in his renowned book *Sharing the Joy of Nature With Children*. The basic idea is that any learning experience works best if the students have their enthusiasm awakened, before their attention is focussed. They then have some kind of direct experience with Nature, which is followed by the opportunity to share that experience with others.

Three of my favourite tools all come from the Wilderness Awareness School in America. The first is the Flow Learning Cycle (a development of 'flow learning'), which begins with the assumption that 'kids don't start the day ready for focussed learning.' The Flow Learning Cycle moves through eight 'directions', marked out in the form of a compass. The first direction (and also the last) is the North East, symbolising the opening and closing of the teaching. The East is next with Inspiration, moving on through Activation in the Southeast; Focussing; Having a break; Gathering and sharing; Reflection, Integration, before returning to the close in the Northeast once more. This teaching cycle is an educational technology, as are the concept of Mentoring and Coyote Teaching, which are the second and third tools respectively. In the introduction to his new 'multi-tool of a book', *Coyotes Guide to Connecting with Nature*, the founder of the W.A.S., Jon Young, describes this way of education as:

"At its very best, Coyote Teaching helps the individuals realise their full potential to the benefit of their community. It consists of a powerful set of tools for coaxing out of individuals what nature has provided and stored away. The mentoring draws people to the edge of their knowledge and experience, and guides them into new territory."

Observing that people have different learning styles has been very useful and exciting as I came upon different models of the various ways people learn. Fleming (*Fleming, N.D. and Mills, C. (1992), Not Another Inventory, Rather a Catalyst for Reflection, To Improve the Academy, Vol. 11, 1992.*) said some people learn either visually, through listening or through being more hands on. There are also, according to Kolb (*Experiential Learning: Experience as the source of learning and development* (1984), Convergers, Divergers, Assimilators and Accommodators. However, finding out that there are about 71 different models of learning styles was more than confusing, and eventually somewhat disappointing as studies showed that there was little evidence to back up the ideas that people fit into neat little boxes labelled with different learning styles! So, what have I learnt from this? One size does not fit all! If at first I don't succeed, I try another way to get the point across, and remember that people learn in their *own* way, in their *own* time.

In my tool bag, I also have some metaphorical WD40 and universal glue. Both are things people have said to me.

The first quote, the WD40, comes from a time when I was feeling disheartened as an environmental educator, and wondering whether anything I was teaching was going in. The person next to me said,

"Being a teacher is like being a rose. You drop petals on the ground, and occasionally someone will pick one up and treasure it."

The glue, that fixes anything, came from a time when I was finishing my degree in Environmental Science, feeling woefully inadequate to the task of being able to do anything positive for the prophesised impending environmental crisis. I went to see a wise elder, Fritjof Capra, giving a lecture at Schumacher College, Devon. After the lecture, I was filled with a longing to at least do something, but what? I knew not! So, I went and asked him. He said, simply,

"Be an example."

And that was that. This book is an example of what I do outdoors, "learning to play, playing to learn", for the greater good of all, I hope.

Why play outdoors?
Mother Nature is the greatest teacher and carer for our offspring and play is the way children learn best. One of our jobs as parents, family members, teachers, forest school leaders and play-workers is to facilitate interaction between our children and Nature, so our children feel at home on the Earth. It is essential for our children to have quality time amongst Nature, for their mental, physical and spiritual development. Children have a deep green affinity to nature, they are internally wired up to learn and play with their environment.

As a race, we humans have spent the vast majority of our time on this planet relating directly, on an everyday living level, with the patterns of natural systems. Our own internal systems and structures are naturally influenced by the glorious and beautiful chaos of Nature. Straight lines, flat surfaces and uniform blocks of colour are human created phenomena and make play spaces that do not encompass the learning requirements of the human whole body, mind and spirit. We need to let our children play out, and not only the young children... there's a lot of teenagers, adults and grandparents that need playtime too!

Who says Grandma's footsteps only played by youngsters – it's serious sneaking practice!

Shelter and fire making – play time for adults under the guise of teambuilding!

There are many books on the market about the intellectual side to the argument that children need be allowed out to play, for their sake, our sake, and the planet's. Richard Louv's book, *Last Child in the Woods: Saving our Children from Nature Deficit Disorder*, has spurred a National Dialogue in the United States among educators, health professionals, parents, developers and conservationists. This influential work about the staggering divide between children and the outdoors links the lack of nature in the lives of today's wired generation to some of the most disturbing childhood trends, such as the rises in obesity, attention disorders, and depression.

In *Coyote's Guide* Jon Young, calls and inspires us, as parents, uncles and aunties, mentors and teachers, to take action, and facilitate interaction with the natural world. To help us all become more 'ecoliterate'. How? By getting out there, playing games, doing activities and perhaps most importantly, sitting still and watching, listening, being, smelling, waiting…., and re-connecting with nature.

So where can we let our kids go out to play? There are a lot of people on this planet. In 2009, for the first time in human history, more people will live in urban, rather than rural settings. In England, every scrap of land is now owned and fenced. For the last 500 years the powerful, the wealthy and the literate have steadily enclosed our ancestral wild places until all we have to romp around on are a few National Parks, footpaths and commons, most of which are subject to various conditions of use and are under great demand from walkers, mountain-bikers, landscape painters and so on. It seems that we, like real life wilderness bushcrafters have to 'do the best we can with what we've got!' It is also worth knowing that in my experience many landowners, if given the respect of simply asking nicely and explaining why, and taking all your rubbish with you when you leave, will kindly grant access to land hitherto deemed 'private' and 'out of bounds'.

Our local wild or wild-ish spaces, like scrubby patches along a footpath, 'waste ground', derelict buildings and even the less kempt parts of a playground are just as important as our National Parks; they offer a chance for children to get closer to Nature. Our children and wild places should be protected from the growing culture of fear, they should saved from being wrapped up in cotton wool, health and safety, fence to fence tarmac and rubber surfacing, and delivered from money hungry land agents and not sold out to 'development' because our children *and* Nature need to be able to grow up properly.

Simply taking young people into nature, whether it is a tiny city park or a National Park, will open their doors of perception. Most young children need little help or encouragement to get involved in play of some kind. For children not used to playing in the great outdoors it's not always easy to engage, but it doesn't usually take long to get the most city hardened boys setting up throwing-stick ranges and even digging their own pitfall traps to catch rabbits!

Nature does the teaching and we adults are the classroom assistants! Often all you need to do as an adult is be there for your children so that they feel safe to play freely, to take a few risks and explore a bit more in the knowledge that you are just a call for help away.

During free and imaginative play children create their own chances to do so many things; from manipulating small objects to increasing their agility, from estimating sizes to creating special places, from working through stress to simply nodding off, feeling safe.

When playing out, sometimes the more primitive and mythological archetypes can be seen in a child's play. 'There may be dragons and wizards in these parts, you know, why, that might even be a...' When we enhance the magic in play, there are wonderful opportunities for sprinkling a little fairy dust (metaphorical and real), doing a little purposeful pixie magic and looking for trolls. Playing in natural places instils a sense of wonder, stimulates inventiveness, ingenuity, problem solving and resourcefulness; playing out can increase physical agility, stamina and a general hardiness. Nimble fingers lead to nimble minds, and the inherent creativity and diversity of Nature infuses children's bodies, minds and spirits with a spell from the sensuous world.

On a final note, a recent study, *'Play, Naturally'*, by Stuart Lester and Martin Maudsley of Playwork Partnerships, comparing playing out in Nature with playing out in man made environments, have shown that playing out in Nature during the early years develop caring attitudes and behaviour towards people and planet later on in life. Can we afford not to facilitate outdoor play in natural places for our children and all our relations?

Chapter 1

What are we and where do we come from?

It's not an easy question to answer! I would like to suggest that we are what we eat, see, and hear. We are more than a simple machine of bone and flesh. We are one whole great big interdependent living system of cells made from earth and water fuelled by magic sparks of sunlight. We are the sum of all our ancestors and influenced by all the stories we have heard. We are also the result of the choices we make.

We are what we eat

From a practical point of view, the food and drinks we consume provide all the building blocks our bodies need to grow. If we eat food that has travelled from New Zealand, we have bits of New Zealand water, soil and sunlight in us. We have the option of being truly home-grown, by only eating locally grown produce, or being at one with the planet by eating produce from all over the world. Our shops provide us with almost anything we want to eat from almost anywhere. Whatever we choose has a noticeable effect on the landscape around us, and sadly we no longer see the effects of many of the consumer choices we make, because many of the goods are produced far away, with 'hidden' consequences. For example, ecosystems in and around some beautiful lakes in Kenya's rift valley are being dramatically altered by the all year round demand and supply for cut flowers in British supermarkets and florist. We get to see the beautiful flowers here, but we don't get to see the lack of worker's rights, the harmful effects of pesticides and fertilisers on humans and wildlife, the carbon dioxide emitted in transport, the pollution of water sources above and below ground (time to grow more flowers at home, I think!).

Talking of things produced far away, sunlight, which plants convert into an energy form we can assimilate, travels about 150 million kilometres. Without that sunlight there would be no collection of cells called 'a human' feeding off different collections of cells called 'plants' and 'animals' whose life processes are also fuelled by sun energy. As the Cuban proverb says,

"When the sun rises, it rises for everyone".

We are the sum total of our ancestors

Every physical thing, from a gas to a stone, has atoms in it. These atoms may last with, or change state through, time. Some scientists will tell us that we are all likely to have at least one atom inside us that was once inside a woolly mammoth. Within every cell of our bodies is a hereditary material, DNA, which gives blueprints for the way a cell looks and works. How it looks and works depends on how it has survived the course of time and place. We are history. We are the legacy of the experience of our ancestors. We have been and continue to be influenced by the patterns of the physical world around us.

Reflections on a lake on a misty, spring morning.

We are body, mind and spirit

It was hard, yet also rather exciting, from me to accept that I am also spirit. The problem was that although I believed we all have a spiritual part to ourselves, I had, until then, no proof. I am, like so many people in the industrialised west, a product of an education system based on a utilitarian worldview, where all of nature is a spiritless source of resources to be exploited for financial reward. Leaving school during the late 80's, studying environmental sciences at university and travelling extensively during the 90's, I found there are many other worldviews and spiritual traditions. The ones that appeal to me most are the more nature based animistic and spiritual beliefs held by the likes of Taoists and hunter-gatherers. Several experiences with plants and animals have clearly shown me that flora and fauna are alive with spirits (more on this later in the wild first aid chapter) as well as Adenosine Tri Phosphate (the chemical considered by biologists as the energy currency of life). Yet it wasn't until I went on a wilderness philosophy course that I realised for myself I am a spirit too.

During the weekend course, we practised expanding our awareness by watching, listening and meditating in Nature. As our minds became calmer and our bodies relaxed, we saw more and more of the comings and goings of nature around us, and within us. One of the exercises involved sending our 'mind's eye' out of our bodies, to travel a short way into the landscape, look at something, and then return. We then had to walk and locate the sight we had seen with our mind's eyes. In other words, we were to travel in spirit to look at something and then to go in the physical to find it. This was the kind of activity I found very challenging, as I wanted to visually see with my mind's eye in techni-colour. What I would normally receive was aching eyeballs, and full volume mind babble. However, I was giving my all to the activities and challenges of the weekend. I did my best to follow the instruction.

During the meditation, I dutifully intended my spirit to travel in the direction I had chosen, while still being unsure I actually had a spirit. A moment later, in my minds eye I saw a small bright blue shape, roughly triangular, against a light, browny-orange background. I intended my spirit to return, and momentarily felt my body shake, ever so slightly, as I turned my awareness to my breath and the beating of my heart.

Larch flowers, in early March are like miniature Chinese temples.

Getting to my feet I walked off in the direction I had sent my spirit. Topping a rise, I looked out into a larch plantation with a sea of bluebells underfoot. Last year's larch needles made a fine, warm and light, browny-orange carpet! I felt momentarily amazed, then suddenly daunted. The prospect of locating the one place I had seen with my mind's eye was completely overwhelming. There were so many bluebells! *'Follow your heart'* – the teachers' words came back to me.

It was then I remembered that the blue I had seen was different to the purplish-blue of the bluebells. It was more of a bright blue. I breathed deeply and set off a bit further, trying to follow a feeling of 'the right way to go'. After about twenty paces I stopped, dumbfounded, because there, lying on a bed of larch needles, was a small, triangular piece of bright blue rubber balloon! From that moment I realised I am more than a mind and a body; I am a spirit too. I also know that if we are all to get on in this world we need be tolerant of different spiritual beliefs, and understanding of the cultural contexts in which we have been brought up, and that my view of the world is not shared by everyone else.

We are what we have been told

By entering the world of the myth and creation stories, we get a glimpse of the time before time, a magical and dreamlike time inhabited by many different spirits and beings, Gods and Goddesses. Creation myths are a part of all human societies on this planet, often explaining how things came to be, setting examples of 'how to behave' and 'what happens if'. Myths and stories are very powerful and have been used by those who wield power to influence others, and I think it is true to say that how we see the world and everything in it depends a lot on the stories we hear as we grow. Stories have power or medicine (borrowing a native American term) and can turn us into all kinds of people.

Mama Africa

This modern story and the suggested accompanying activity will help people to see that whatever religion, race or creed we are, we are all made from the earth and things that grow or live on the earth.

Once upon a time Mama Africa was sitting all alone in the plains, dreaming and breathing, dreaming and breathing. There were no animals then, no insects buzzing around. No creepies crawling. No lions roaring, (this is a good moment to involve your listeners and ask them to suggest animals to which you can add a verb)... As the sun warmed the earth and the rains watered the land all kinds of plants grew up around Mama Africa, and she gazed at them in wonder.

One day Mama Africa pushed her strong hands down into the friendly earth around her and felt around. She felt something cool, moist and squidgy. When she pulled her hands back out she had some clay in them. She loved the clay and made all kinds of shapes from it. Into the clay she stuck different shaped parts from the plants around her...seeds, buds, branches and twigs. Onto the clay she pressed all kinds of colours and patterns from the plants and rocks.

After she had finished each creation, she put it in the sun to dry. When they were all dry, Mama Africa gave each of them a name and breathed on them. The clay figures came to life and went off to live amongst the plants, walking on the land, flying through blue skies and digging burrows into the earth. And that's how it came to be that all the animals and people came to live in Africa, and some say, that deep in the rainforest she is still there, making new creatures every day.

Blobsters
All ages
Group size: Any
At least 15 mins

Ready

Once upon a time, Gordon MacLellan, an inspirational environmental educator, gave me a small lump of clay. He prompted us to make a round ball with the clay and then turn it into a 'somebody'. He suggested we start by looking for something with which to make the eyes... seed pods, seeds, sticks with buds on the end... anything that takes your fancy, and then fix them into or onto the blob. And so a blobster was born!

Blobster making is an incredibly versatile activity of which I never get bored. It's a chance to play God, to make creatures of your wildest imagination, and to remember that our bodies are all made of the earth, and the beings that live and grow on it.

Blobsters can be any shape you like, can have as many eyes, arms, legs, hair, spines, wings, teeth, heads as you like - the opportunities are endless and change with the environment and the seasons.

If you want to use soft stemmed flowers, like daisies, as eyes, then try making a hole with a little twig in the blob first, then poke in the flower stem. Use hidden sticks to pin blobs together. Wrap clay around twigs to make snakes and other kinds of long thin blobsters.

Remember to have respect for everything you use or pick. The way I say this is to say something like, "There are Nature Spirits in everything. We need to say thank you to each one before we pick something from Nature to stick into the clay". For older age groups I tell them a wise saying I heard from my childhood in Africa that "every tree has a spirit that the careful listener can hear and understand". It follows that every plant has a spirit, and it may be wise to give thanks for the things they provide. Sometimes, to emphasise the point, I slap a blob onto the bark of a tree and make the face of a spirit as suggested by the tree, pressing in leaves as hair. While modelling, I talk about the green man, the Celtic protector of the wyldwood, reminding listeners of the more animist, pre-Christian roots of this green and pleasant land.

Get set

You will need blobs of clay or sticky mud (from a riverbank, a hole in the garden, a bag of clay from the pottery suppliers) and some natural objects to stick into the blob.

Go!

"Come on in everyone, let's make a toe-to-toe circle." A toe-to-toe circle is way of getting people to stand in a circle without having to hold hands - they arrange themselves with their toes and outsides of the feet/shoes touching, instead.

"We are going to make bloblsters. Blobsters are characters made from blobs of clay with bits of nature stuck into them." Taking some clay off the lump, (or out of the bag), I start by making a demo blobster, often telling the Mama Africa story at the same time.

Hand out blobs, and guard the clay from people wanting to make herds of blobsters.

Children love to name their blobsters, give them a home or make up lives for their blobster, so round off the session with a circle time, and then everyone gets the chance to share the name of their blobster and show it to the group. If there is time, each person can say a little more.

Chapter 2

Survival Basics

Being able to make your own shelter, light a fire, prepare water for drinking and find something to eat are the basic skills of life. When people develop these skills, they feel more at home upon the Earth and good in themselves; they have self-esteem, a certain 'I can take care of myself' attitude. Learning survival skills can also be very humbling when, for example, you have to kill another animal to survive.

Survival skills put us in touch with the forces of nature. We can appreciate the powers of the elements and our own ability to live amongst them when we are close to nature. Slashing rain and buffeting winds are far more real when experienced from a rain-tight and cosy shelter that we have built ourselves.

This chapter is not meant to turn you into a Ray Mears or Bear Grylls over a weekend. It contains playful activities that introduce and put into practice some of the fundamental elements of survival skills, namely shelter building, fire making, finding and preparing water, and knowing what you can eat.

Shelter Building

Blobster Dens
Age 3-103
At least 30 mins
At least one leader for every 15 students.

Ready
Blobster dens are small shelters built to house blobsters and they take all kinds of shapes and sizes. It is really beneficial to start small, making mini shelters for little characters, so that building techniques can be learned with minimum effort, maximum experience, before moving onto 'full' sized shelters.

The drive to make dens is instinctive. A basic need is fulfilled in gathering materials at hand to make a den, a hide or hideout, a home for the night, or a longer-term shelter for the kids to play in through the summer. It is also great fun and very absorbing. It is so easy to spend anything from half an hour to a whole day on the activity.

Children learn a lot from watching others as they play. I find the best way to share ideas is simply to start making a shelter myself.

"Chris, what do you think of when building a shelter?" I think of:

What am I going to use the shelter for?
Where am I going to make it?
What materials are close at hand?
What will I use for the framework?
Where should I have the entrance?
Is water or wind going to flow into it?
How will I keep the rain out?
How to insulate it with and how to keep the draughts out?
Could anything fall on my den while I am in it/Is it safe?
Will it have an impact on animal route ways and habitats?

I also decide whether to have a fire or not (for overnighters the answer is usually yes!).

In the interests of using my own energy reserves and the resources the landscape presents efficiently, I want to build a shelter with the least expenditure of my energy. To save brainpower the shapes and patterns around me always influence me. I also want it to be cheap on energy to light and heat, so (as architects could do, but so often don't seem to in real life houses), I can face the shelter towards the sun to maximize the 'solar gain'. The resulting shelter depends very much on the time, the place and the materials that come readily to hand. It usually blends into the surrounding landscape.

Chris Drury is one of the people by whom I am very inspired, and whose book, *Found Moments in Time and Place*, I often show children before we start making dens. Chris is a land artist working with nature, whose work explores nature and culture, both inner and outer. Children love the way his shelters are built utilizing what there is in the nearby landscape. Here is an example of one of the person-sized shelters he made one winter:

The final thing to know is that houses and shelters vary so much across the world depending on what kind of landscape these have been built in. The book I use to show examples of different houses from around the world is *Shelter*, by Lloyd Kahn. From igloos to tropical tree houses, from adobe to cob, all our early building styles and materials are a product of the land they come from. The same goes for the dens you make with the children. They will vary enormously. Our skill as facilitators lies in helping the children to make real the dens they are imagining, to draw on our own experience of working with natural materials to pull out of the bag, so to speak, the den of their dreams, without taking over.

So, to arm you with some shelter building skills I present you three ancient secrets of ninja shelter building! (Just kidding about the ancient ninja bit):

First, **the forked stick**. They are so useful as these photos show...

A tripod of three

supporting a horizontal pole

Two short forks holding a longer one

Two uprights holding up a beam

Four upright forks, two beams and three (only two visible) forks as roof timbers placed with forks on the lower roof beam - on the right.

Second: **using foliage as waterproofing**. The main thing to remember is start from the bottom of the structure and work up, using more than you need in case it rains, (or someone comes along with a watering can to test it!!

Finally: **plod**. Plod? Plod is anything gooey that can be used like a mortar to stick things together or smear over structures to fill up holes and cracks, to keep the wind out, that kind of thing. All you need is some water, some earth and some fibrous material to make a simple kind of plod. Stomp on it and squish it to mix it all up and splat it on in globs!

Get set

You will need some blobsters to make dens for, some material for structures like sticks and stones, some materials for tiling, shingling or waterproofing and some materials for insulating. It depends on where you are as to what you make. A watering can with or without water in it can also provide a great incentive to get a cover over the blobster... just the threat of 'rain' is often enough to inspire your shelter builders into action!

Go!

"Now we are going to make some dens for our blobsters to live in. If the dens are just big enough for the blobsters to fit in, the blobsters will find it easier to keep warm, and you will have to collect less materials to make the den." Give a few quick demos of using materials found in the chosen location, and show a few of the things that can be done with forked sticks.

"It is your turn to make dens now. Let's work in small groups and teams. You can have (for example) up to 4 people in each team. You can work on your own if you want, too."

Help as little as possible, but as much as they need! Ask leading questions like "Have you tried blowing on your den to see if it stays up when the wind blows?" "Have you spotted those sticks over there?", "Is it rainproof?" and "How does your blobster stay warm?"

Make lots of site visits too, since children love adults being interested in what they are doing. I encourage the builders to go around and have a look at each other's structures, both during the construction phase and when time is up or the job is done, whichever comes first.

A blobster hotel!

If there is time to do so, it is worth visiting each den as a whole group. Facilitating an appraisal of each den, by asking questions like "What do you like about this den?" help the group focus on the positives, makes the builders feel good and draws out some of the learning objectives. Finish by asking the groups whether they want to leave their blobster dens up, with blobster inside, or whether they want to demolish the dens! If they want to demolish the dens, I encourage people to put the larger objects, like stones, logs and branches back where they found them, because they were probably someone else's home and habitat before they became building materials.

Seeing where the blobsters live...the final site visits and group evaluation in process.

Fire and Fire-Making!

We are fascinated by fire. It's such a primal elemental force, and it makes us human. No other creature uses fire like we humans do. I bet you could think of 20 things you use some form of fire for in your everyday life right now…go on…dare ya!

My list of suggestions is at the back of the book ;-)

Children love to learn about fire and making fire. So much so that, if they are not facilitated to do so by adults, some kids will go off and teach themselves about fire, and this is when accidents are more likely to happen.

Becoming a fire starter

It is the aim of this section to share a few ways of going about making fires, while developing safety awareness and respect for fire. Fire-craft is knowing what kind of fire to use for a particular purpose.

It is healthy for children to develop a respectful relationship with fire from an early age. My daughter has been able to 'play' lighting matches, as long as an adult was around, from about three years old and now, at nine years old, competently lights the wood stove at home. The earlier a child learns to be aware of the dangers of fire and behaves sensibly around a fire the better.

To begin, a box of matches and a newspaper is all you need. Learning how to strike a match and keep it alight in a breeze is quite a skill for the uninitiated. Fine motor skills are developed and fears overcome. It is almost a rite of passage for a small person to feel comfortable about holding a fire in their hands, albeit on a match,

Useful things to know

There are several ways to light a fire, including frictional (rubbing sticks together), mechanical (fire piston), chemical (potassium permanganate and glycerine), and electrical methods (9V battery and wire wool) as well as focusing sunlight. All fires require oxygen, fuel and heat to keep going.

Basic match rules

- Strike away from yourself and others.
- Holding the match like you would a dart means you strike along the axis of strength of the match, so it is least likely to break. Once the match is alight the middle finger is removed from the matchstick, the matchbox quickly put in a pocket, so that both hands can be cupped round the flame to protect it from any wind.

- Strike the match close to the combustible material, so there is less chance of the match going out in the wind as you move the match to set the material alight
- Heat goes up so hold the match almost put the flame beneath the combustible material.
- Pushing matches *into* the combustible material makes them go out!

Some definitions:

Ember

An ember is a glowing coal of material, usually carbon, like wood or coal. An ember is used to create fire, as in fire by friction, or is left over at the end of the fire, and can be found in the ashes, before all the heat is lost from the fire.

Tinder

Tinder is any easily combustible material that can be used to get a fire going by simple methods, such as using an ember, spark or match. It tends to be fluffy or fibrous, offering a large surface area for the fire to catch on to. Examples include, silver birch bark, dried leaves, grass and flowers, pine needles, cotton, char cloth, frayed rope, thin rubber strips as well as dry fluff and receipts from your pocket! Tinder is used to light kindling, which in turn is used to set light to larger pieces of wood like logs.

Kindling
Kindling is thin dead, dry plant stems, sticks or splinters of wood, anything from pencil lead thinness to pencil thickness.

Standing dead wood.
This is dead wood that has not yet come in contact with the ground, so is air dried, and most suitable for lighting fires. You can tell if wood is dead by scratching off the outer layer of bark – if it is green underneath, the wood is still alive! Dead wood is also vital habitat for mini-beasts, so make sure you leave some behind. *Encourage and be an example of being 'frugal with firewood' – only generate the light, heat and company you need!*

Fire pit
A fire pit should be at least a foot in diameter and clear to bare earth, with a shallow bowl-like base. With a bowl-like bottom, the flammable material tends to move to the bottom of the pit, and not roll out. A handy stick or stone is usually enough to do the digging, where needed.

It is important to clear to bare earth for many reasons:

- To see if you might destroy anyone's home- there might be woodlice, mouse holes, bumblebee nests...it's nice to check and if so, try somewhere else.
- To temporarily move the turf, so you do don't leave a scorch mark directly on the surface of the ground when you leave.
- To check how damp the ground is.
- To see if there are any stones which might explode on heating. Any stones that are non-calcareous (chalky or lime-stony), like flint for example, may explode when either the water in the stone turns to gas forcing the stone apart, or when the matter of the rock expands suddenly due to the molecules inside the rock getting excited by the fire's energy.
- In peaty soil the fire can spread through rich organic matter in the ground, so if you find peat (a soft, very dark almost black soil) where you want to lay a fire, try somewhere else, like sandy patches or gravelly stream edges.

Fire Safety

When doing fire activities make sure you have a bucket or two of water about – for putting out fires and for cooling any small minor burns. Any minor burns larger than a postage stamp should have medical attention. Don't burst any blisters, or cover the burn with anything fluffy, adhesive or oily.

Keep a large wool or fire blanket handy. One of the best ways to put out the flames on someone whose clothes are on fire is to stop them panicking and running around (wrap them tightly in a blanket if you have one handy) drop them to the ground, and roll them along the ground until the flames are smothered.

Clothing guidelines

The best clothing material to wear around fire is wool as it is the least flammable of the commonly worn fabrics. The next best is cotton, then hemp and linen. Synthetic fibres are the least preferable as they can melt when a spark lands on them, and burn at high temperatures when alight.

Warn people who are wearing synthetic or loose clothing to take extra care when close to flames and sparks. Ask people who have long or frizzy hair to tie it up or tidy it away in a hat.

Making Sparks to Light Tinder
Age 6 upwards
Group size: one leader for 10 students.
15 – 30 mins

Ready

When children have developed enough strength and motor skills, it can be very rewarding and magical to learn to use a firesteel.

What is a fire steel? Originally developed for the Swedish Department of Defence, the Swedish Firesteel is a flash of genius. Its 3,000°C spark makes fire building easy in any weather, at any altitude. Used by a number of armies around the world, the firesteel's dependability has already made it a favourite of survival experts, hunters, fishermen and campers. It has also found its way into cabins and backyards as a foolproof way to light stoves and gas-barbecues. There are now many versions of the firesteel, containing a mixture of 7-20 different metals. They are readily available at various outdoor shops.

Cotton wool, preferably organic if you can get it, is the best material with which to practise making sparks to ignite tinder.

A spark is produced when the firesteel is scraped across a sharp steel edge, like the back of a knife blade or a metal file. Most firesteels are supplied with a steel strike.

There are so many things to learn about fire that this simple fifteen minute activity can be repeated again and again with youngsters.

Get set

Set up some fireproof hearths – do this yourself or build it into the activity. A hearth can be as simple as clearing a small area to bare earth…sweeping away the leaf litter till you get to the soil is easy enough. I have also used small paving slabs, which give a slightly raised, defined area to work on. Effective, safe, but not very bushcrafty! You will also need some tinder, and to begin with cotton wool perfect.

Go!

"This is a fire steel and this is the striker. As I push the striker into and along the edge of the firesteel it gives off a small shower of sparks, like this…" (Wow! Ooooh! Ahh!...that kind of thing is heard from the audience!).

"When sparks are directed at a suitable tinder, they are so hot it sets it on fire, like this".

"In a moment I am going to hand out some firesteels and cotton wool. There will be one firesteel per hearth. When it is your turn, make sure you strike downwards, onto the tinder, and on the hearth."

Hand out the firesteels and small quantities of cotton wool at a time. Be ready to give assistance and make sure that people are using the correct side of the striker and always work at their hearth.

'Fire weed'- excellent tinder. A tinder bundle up close. Pine Needles

Flaming Fire Pits!
Ages 6 and up
Group size: up to 35
About 45 mins

Ready

This activity is for learning about how to collect and prepare tinder, igniting it with a single spark and making a small fire. Finding out what turns a spark into flames, and small flames into a fire, is best done through repetitive play. So, now you and your students are successful, almost every time, with the fire steel and cotton wool, it's time to move on to learning about other tinders.

Get set

Choose an environment that potentially offers many different natural tinders – a woodland edge habitat is likely to offer more diversity than a single species conifer wood for example. Bring along some kind of "bag of wonderous fluff" containing natural tinders you have previously collected and dried. Have cotton wool ready too, just in case. Bring along fire steels, and marshmallows to toast later if you want to let the group have some, because they will almost always want to get a small fire going at the end of their experimentation.

Go!

"The next activity is called 'flaming fire pits!' The first thing to do is create a fire pit to work in, or series of mini fire pits, one for each tinder. Define a working area, usually circular, by scratching the earth with a stick, to keep people who are not in your group, out."

Make sparks to ignite a few natural tinders, one by one, asking questions about the common properties of the tinders; the dryness, the fluffiness and if it is made up of many fibres.

"Working in small groups of up to 5 people, I want everyone to create a small fire pit, or series of smaller mini fire pits to do your tinder research in. Then you can go off and hunt for materials you think will make good tinders. When each team returns, I will give them a fire steel. The boundaries for the search are...(define you boundaries!). Later we will gather again to see the results of our research."

Tinders, clockwise from top left, birch bark, western red cedar inner bark, lime bark, King Alfred's cakes, Reed mace seeds, clematis seeds

"Okay everyone, off you go!' Try to find at least four different tinders that work well."

When a group returns give them a fire steel, explaining that the firesteels should stay in the circle around the fire pit, to stop them getting lost in the woods. Let them have a go at seeing what 'catches a fire' and what doesn't. Groups can have their own fires as appropriate (perhaps with some marshmallows to toast), if it fits in with the flow of the session.

We finish off the activity by asking everyone to bring the materials they have experimented with together. We make two piles, ones that catch a spark and those that don't. I add tinders collected previously to the 'pile that does', and then we all have a chance to see and remind ourselves of the properties of materials suitable for fire making.

Five-Minute Fire Challenge.
Suitable for ages 5 and up
Time 1-1.5hrs with 4 groups
Group size: 2-35

Ready
In order to set a context and provide an objective to lighting a fire in five minutes I set a scenario where someone has fallen into some water and is now cold and wet. He needs warming up, drying off and returning home before dark. Our groups then have five minutes to prepare everything needed to get a fire going. As one large group, we travel from hearth to hearth to watch and learn as each small group rises to the challenge.

Get set
Choose a suitable area to work in. Divide your party into small groups (3-6 people in each is best). Provide each group with some dry tinder to get a fire going - a sheet of newspaper for novices and a handful of straw or dry cleavers for the more advanced students.

You will also need a bucket or two of water, for putting out the fires at the end, and just in case anyone burns themselves.

Go!
"Who wants to do the five minute fire challenge? We will be establishing small fires and you have a time limit to do it in. What do we need to do before lighting a fire?"

Hopefully the responses that include 'collect all the materials' and 'make a fire place'. Remind people to clear to bare ground in their chosen fireplace - to check for insect nests, stones that might explode, etc.

"Imagine this. It is a cold wintery day. You are going exploring with your mates and one of them falls into the river you are trying to cross. You want to get a hot fire going as quick as possible to warm them up and dry their clothes, before moving on. Between you, you have some dry paper and a box of matches (or a fire steel and tinder depending on their ability)."

They will be itching to go by now.

"You have five minutes to **gather and prepare** all the materials you need to light a fire. You **do not get to light** your fires yet!"

I then run about and try to collect everything for my own fire (although sometimes I have gathered and stashed materials in a Blue Peter fashion). When five minutes or thereabouts is up it's time to call everybody in. As a whole group, we then visit each fire in turn to see how the teams get on lighting their fires.

As each group has its turn, ask several question before the first match is lit:

- "What do you like about this fire?"
- "Who thinks it will light? And why?"

Let each group decide who will go first, and they get one match per person to try lighting the fire. As each person has a go and we are watching the match being applied to the fire I ask, "What can we learn from this?"

By the time every group has had a go we should have learnt something, even if we haven't got any fires lit!

The things we usually find out are:

- The flames on a match only set fire to things that are above or to the side of the flames
- Matches go out if pushed into dense tinder
- Newspaper doesn't burn well if scrumpled up too tightly
- Tinder gets damp if left on the ground for too long
- Tinder with too much air in it goes up in a 'whoof'
- Air contains oxygen which helps fires grow
- Tinder with no air just smoulders if it burns at all
- Thin sticks catch alight quicker than fat sticks
- Tinder that is concentrated in one place works better to form a heart for the fire
- A fire needs a heart to grow
- Tinder stacked vertically creates a thermal column, where warm air, rising from the lit tinder below, dries out and heats the tinder above, making it easier to catch light
- Several grades of wood are needed for a successful fire
- A little raft of wood helps air get to the bottom of the fire
- Using a windbreak of some sort can help on windy days because too much air blows small fires out
- A little extra breath into the fire can help on calm days
- Fires poked by sticks can lose heart and go out.

When it comes to your turn make sure you can give a good demo, so practise beforehand! Keep a bail of straw in the shed for rainy days and a selection of thoroughly dry tinders and fire lighting kit in a sturdy drybag (store it open in an airing cupboard if you have one, because matches, for example will draw in the damp, even if stored in a waterproof bag, when left in a shed for a month or two over winter). When you have done your demonstration, let the groups have another go and do your best to help each group light a small fire.

Useful things to know for a successful demonstration

A good start: From the bottom up, bundles of cleavers, nettle stalks, beech and birch twigs, beech and birch sticks.

Collect at least three bundles of pencil-lead-thin twigs or dried plant stems, slightly thicker twigs and then finger thick twigs. Each bundle should look like a mini witches broom and be about 30cm/12inches long, so you can hold one end of the bundle, while positioning the other end over the hottest part of the tinder.

It's often easiest to collect branches, take them to the fireplace, and then break and sort them into bundles.

Place a few finger-thick or slightly thicker sticks in the centre of your fireplace first, like a little raft to start your fire on. As mentioned earlier, this helps get the fire off damp ground and enables air to flow into the base of the fire.

Light your tinder. Hold the two bundles of kindling so that they cross, one above the other, above the flames, lightly so as not to crush the young fire, allowing it to 'breathe', and create a tall thermal column for the hot air to travel through. Get the next bundle on as soon as you can, gently. By this stage, there should be a visibly impressive fire going, generating a very reasonable amount of heat and tall flames. Add increasingly large pieces of wood to the fire.

We usually finish the challenge with a practice session, where the teams have a chance to consolidate their newly gained knowledge and have success at lighting a fire in their own time. Before we leave site I make sure everyone extinguishes their fires, cleans out the fire pits, and leave nothing but footprints.

The seed head of clematis makes acceptable, if slightly 'spitty' tinder.

Water

Widgeon landing on water.

A South African proverb states: "The old elephant knows where to find water". As we grow in understanding of Nature we begin to know where to find water, often by knowing what kinds of plants and birds live in wet places. We can then track the water through patterns of plant life and birdsong across the landscape.

Wild and pure water is full of life and vibrational beauty. If you have ever drunk from a pure, clean mountain spring you will know what I mean, and what a completely different experience it is to drinking city tap water. Masaru Imoto, in his book *Messages from Water*, has shown just how much the quality of wild water differs from water in man made watercourses with pictures taken of ice crystals from mountain streams and city rivers. The difference is astonishing.

Snowflakes on buddleia leaves.

Water is purified naturally through the water cycle. Excited water molecules evaporate from the ground and large bodies of water and transpire through minute holes in the leaves of green plants to form water vapour. When this vapour cools, it condenses to form clouds and returns to earth as rain, hail and snow.

Once earthbound, the water can find itself stored as ice or snow, it can flow over the surface in rivers, or flow down through the soil to become groundwater. As water filters down through layers of soil and permeable rock (porous rock through which water can flow), it is often cleaned of the particulate matter it might be carrying. While in contact with the rocks, minerals and chemical ions dissolve in the water, giving that particular water its unique taste and pH (its point on a scale expressing acidity and alkalinity).

Spring water and well water was once the purest most desirable and revered of water. These water sources are still often referred to as Sacred, and some have genuine medicinal and healing properties, partly I believe because the water comes from deep in the ground and is purified by the Earth, may be rich in minerals and also because of the Spirit of Place, or Genius loci, generated by the thanksgiving, belief and prayer of people visiting the site. Honouring wells and springs is a practice that has slipped by the wayside as people have moved into houses with taps. In my experience, springs and wells really benefit from being celebrated and honoured. The spirit of the place is cheered up and the water tastes better! Why not go on an outing to celebrate a spring near you someday?

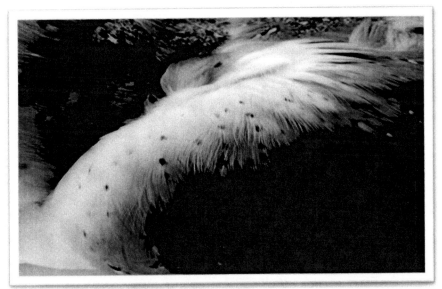
Not a waterfall, but feathers, flowing water-like, on a barn owl's wing.

Sadly, nowadays, a vast array of chemicals and antibiotics produced by humans is finding its way into rivers, water deep underground, high in the mountains and at the bottom of the oceans. Sacred wells and springs do not remain unaffected. Belief and prayer is not enough to solve these problems. We have to be more and more aware of what is 'clean' water, where to find it and how help our earth's water cycle do its cleaning (one way is to put the least amount of harmful chemicals into the water cycle). I am also not saying that any water in any wild place, far away from humans, will be unpolluted - we only need to look to the spread of radio active rain as far as Ireland from the Ukrainian Chernobyl disaster in 1986 to know that pollution knows no boundaries. I am saying that we need to be wary, not only of where our water comes from, but how we put affect the global as 'What goes around, comes around'.

To make 'wild' water (water that hasn't come through a processing plant and a tap) safely drinkable, it often needs to be boiled to kill off wee beasties living in it, like some kinds of protozoa and bacteria, that might do damage to our internal systems. Boiling and processing water alters the minute structural qualities of water and so it is good to consider why and when we should purify water. Water boiling at 100 degrees Celsius ruptures the cell walls of living organisms. At sea level, a rolling boil for a minute should be enough to kill all life in the water, but the higher you go the longer you will need to boil the water. This is because water boils at a lower temperature the higher you go, because the atmospheric pressure keeping the water molecules in a liquid state reduces. Boiling may not kill viruses or remove any chemical toxicity in the water, which is why filtration and chemical processing may be necessary too.

However, before we can make water ready to drink, we have to know where to find it! In order to do that, we need to know the sights and sounds that give us clues to where water is. One way to do this is to go on an Elephant walk.

Elephant Walk
Suitable for groups of up to 16 people.
Ages 4-11
2hrs-6hrs

Ready
I like to take people on a walk, a water-hunting walk. With children, it is easy to pretend you are the old elephant teaching the youngsters about where to find water, and they all follow along trumpeting and raising their pretend trunks!

The basic idea of this activity is to walk through different watery habitats until you get to a place where you can dig your own waterhole, also known as a gypsy well. Plan your route. If possible, choose a route that takes you near a pond, by a river, and ends up in some damp, marshy or waterlogged fields, an ideal place to make a waterhole. You can often tell a field that gets waterlogged sometime in the year, because there will be *Juncus sp* rushes growing in them.

To help your group get familiar with the plants living in water rich environments, prepare a few observational activities to do along the way and while you are at the waterhole waiting for water to seep in, like drawing, leaf rubbing, taking photos (real and pretend).

Get set
You will need a spade, folding shovel or digging stick, clear plastic bottle and a cup. You could also bring a funnel or jug, or as I sometimes do, cut the top off another plastic bottle to use as a funnel. You could also bring some plastic sheeting to keep the area around the hole you dig a bit less trampled.

Go!
"Now we are going on an 'elephant walk'."

"What's that?"

"In some parts of the world people and animals sometimes have to fetch water to drink from wells and waterholes far away from where they live. Some elephants living in the drier parts of Africa will travel hundreds of miles to find water. Today we will be going only a short way to find places where water is found naturally. When we find the right place, we are going to dig our own mini well."

Once sure everybody has got enough clothes, snacks and water for the outing, we set off. At a suitable spot along the way, stop and ask the group about what kinds of things water is used for in our everyday lives and get them to guess what kind of percentage of our bodies are made of water (anywhere from 55-80% depending on age and body size). Talk a little about the water cycle, or perhaps tell a story about a raindrop travelling from sky to sea and back again, which of course is the same thing…but sometimes stories are better holding a group's attention than talks or conversations.

Having arrived at the chosen wet area, we gather round, and dig a hole about 2 feet deep by 2 feet wide. If the water table, the surface below which the ground is wholly saturated with water, is lower than 2 feet, dig deeper! Store the turf and soil neatly nearby. When we are done, I tell them that this is how country folk could find enough to drink in a place where there was no water running along the surface.

"This kind of well is sometimes called a gypsy well. The plants living around here tell up this is a good place to try digging. Water seeps in from the soil around the hole. We will collect it later. So let's go and do something else while we are waiting for our well to fill." If we have chosen your place well, (forgive the pun) water *will* seep out of the soil into the hole you have made, and bingo! A waterhole!

When we all get back to the waterhole, there should be some water in the bottom that can be scooped out with the cup and poured into the clear plastic bottle. I like to point out that in an emergency I could suck the water out with a straw, made from a hollow stem from non-toxic plant. When we have filled the bottle as much as possible, I lift it up for all to see.

"Let's have a look!"

"Is there any water in there?"

There are now more questions to ask:

- How clear is it?
- Would you drink it?
- What could you do to make it drinkable?
- How would you get it out of the waterhole without a cup?
- How could we filter it?

One of the answers to the last question is that you can simply pour water onto the soil around the hole and wait for it to seep into the hole again, which I find is a great way to lead into talking about the underground part of the water cycle, and how water is filtered in the ecosystem by soil and rocks in the ground. It's then time to fill in the hole carefully and walk home, either with the water you have collected to boil up at home, or not!

Filtering Water with Rubbish
Ages 7 and up
Group size: up to 16
About an hour

Ready
Plastic bottles, bags and old clothes are the tools for this next activity. In order to separate out the finer particulate matter from muddy water you can either wait for all the dust to settle, or filter it. This activity is about trial and error, finding out what kinds of readily available rubbish and natural materials we can use to make an effective filter. It's best done on a hot day for reasons that will become obvious, and the activity lends itself to a bit of healthy competition too.

Get set
Collect some old drinks bottles, 1 -2 litres in volume, at least 2 per group, some plastic bags, old plant pots...anything that can be used as a container. Cut off the tops of some of the bottles so they can be used as scoops and funnels. Each group will need one bottle with 1litre marked clearly on it. Have some buckets of (as near as possible) identically muddy water – one between two groups is enough. A couple of filters from home - fish-tank sponges, domestic water filter cartridges, survival water filters for example. Also, have some piles of sand, some string, stones and rubble, smooth leaves,

hairy leaves, grass and old clothes nearby. Jeans and t-shirts are best. Picture of various filters can also be used to promote discussion

Go!

"Everyone in a circle please! Let's separate you into small groups by giving each of you a water sound."

I then go round the circle whispering a water sound into each person's ear. If I want four groups I repeat the sounds every fourth person: "Splash", "drop", "trickle", "drip", "Splash", "drop" etc.

"Ok. There are four different water sounds. Making the sounds I have just given you to, listen for others making the same sound to get into your new groups!"

Once the noise has subsided, explain the principles of filtration.

"Filtration is the process of physically or mechanically separating fluids from solids. Here are some real life examples I have brought from home. In a survival situation, we have to do the best we can with what we've got...from the things around us to the clothes we are wearing. Here we have sand, old clothing, leaves etc for you to use to make some filters. You can use the plastic bottles and bags to make filters in if you like. I want you to collect the clearest litre of water you can in one of these bottles. Good luck!"

Depending on the age of the participants some prompting may be needed and the activity can be more play based or more hypothesis and design based. The final test involves seeing which group has collected the clearest litre of water.

I like to gather the groups and ask:
- Which filter worked best and why?
- What can we learn from this?
- Can we drink it yet? If not, why not?

Useful things to know

Often, the best filter is simply a pair of jeans, one leg inside the other, tied off at the bottom with a knot or some string.

Re-cap and explore the topic a little further by asking a few more questions like:
- What kinds of things can't be filtered out?
- How much water do we all need to drink a day? (At least a litre is good – some say two).
- How is our water purified before it gets to our taps?
- What diseases can be carried by water?
- How can we purify the water further? (By distillation, but this water is so pure that it leaches minerals out of the body, so is actually dangerous to drink it regularly and in large amounts!)

Making Herbal Infusions

Age: any

Group of up to 8-10 per leader (so obviously depends on how many leaders there are and also the size of kettles/teapots/cups you have!)

30 mins

A Kelly or storm kettle, and nettle tea made in a coconut shell cup.

Ready

Making tea is a great way to learn about why we need to boil water and to find out what different herbs taste like.

Herbs have many healing properties, some of which are released in hot water, making an infusion.

By picking fresh herbs we get to see, smell, touch and feel the plant. Each plant has its own spirit. A whole body experience with a plant is more likely to be remembered, and make future relationships with the plant more possible than using herbs bought in packets or ready prepared herb teas. I like to guide someone through an intimate identification process, where they are able to hold, sniff, inspect and give thanks. I present a wide variety of information about a plant too, including medicinal and practical uses if I know any. Five minutes later, they may not remember everything, but will have a memory of that which will enable them to correctly identify it later and maybe remember one fact about the plant next time they come upon it.

As far as I can tell, all young children like making tea and playing with tea sets – probably because their parents drink so much. English people are 'always' making tea and having a chat. For some, tea drinking can be a more formal affair - the Japanese people have a traditional tea ceremony where tasting is done in respectful silence, to be followed later by conversation and chatter. All in all, making brews and potions is one of the oldest rituals we humans have and it can be fun to act up this activity, especially if you have an old tea set in a hamper for a quaint approach, or maybe some form of cloak or wizard costume lurking in the cupboard for a more mystical tack!

Get set

You will need something to carry water in, something to boil the water in, a fire to boil the water on, some cups and some kind of freshly picked herb. Extras include teapot, tea towels to lay everything out on, cucumber sandwiches…oops, getting carried away.

Peppermint is a good choice of herb to begin with, as are wild water-mints, which can often be found in wetland areas. Ground ivy and fennel are also suitable, and so are nettles if you are happy handling them.

A Kelly kettle is ideal for this activity as the water boils quickly and your group can be involved in collecting all the thin sticks to fuel the fire, and then timing how long the water takes to boil. A Kelly or storm kettle is basically a chimney with a water jacket around it. Have a look at the one in the photo… the fire is made at the bottom and comes up through he hole in the middle. The water goes in and then out of the spout on the side.

Go!

"For our next activity we are going to make some tea using fresh leaves from these herbs. Here is the kettle we are going to use. What do we need to make tea?"

"Ok. Let's fill up the kettle with clear stream water, (or use tap water I have carried with me). We also need to establish a fire circle, go through fireside rules, and get a fire going to pop the kettle on."

Three green logs pointing into the fire can be used as a tripod to rest the kettle on because they will burn slower than the dry, dead wood. While the water is boiling and the group is sitting down, hand out cups and pass round the bunch of peppermint so they can pick off a few leaves and put them in their cups. Arrange each cup so that when it comes to pouring the boiled water there is no risk of the water getting on the students or the cups tipping over.

When the water begins boiling, start counting "1,000, 2,000, 3,000…" Sometimes the group joins in. If they do, I carry on. If they don't, I stop! A minute is up. I then ¾ fill the cups and leave them where they are for a few minutes, so that the flavour infuses and the water cools to sipping temperature.

As we sip out tea, remind everyone to experience the tea with all their senses, and remind them to ask themselves questions like:

- "What colour is it?
- How does it smell?
- How does it taste?
- How does the tea make you feel?"

When all the sipping is done, the leaves can be eaten or placed somewhere to decompose naturally, the fire put out, sticks and ashes scattered, and the fire circle returned to its original state. Pack up and move on!

"Hmmm, enough tea... I think it's about time I found something to eat. Let's have a look..."

Food!

It's not so easy to see the hidden impact on our local environment of large scale commercial growing, and the transport systems used to get food into most of our shops. The web of interactions, causes and effects, can baffle even the most complex modelling systems used to predict the outcomes of our current patterns of consumption. Reading the papers and surfing the net I have no clear idea whether my choices are actually causing the environment and the global climate to change.

However, it's easy to see the impact of our eating habits when we are out browsing and foraging. Imagine, that Spring is with us at last. The dog's mercury is just sprouting, there's a smell of wild garlic in the air and the blackbirds are looking ever so smart as they sing to claim territory and mate.

One of my first foraging rituals of the year is to get down on all fours, pick and munch a primrose flower. So soft on the tongue! I am filled with a delicate joy and an expectancy of warmer days. I am reminded of the sound of bumblebees and yummy fresh greens to eat on the wayside. With warm sun on your face, and the smell of daffodils on the air can you think of a better way to enjoy fresh flowers and vegetables? I can't.

The first offerings from spring plants are one of the greatest gifts the earth has to offer. No, I am not an herbivore or a strict veggie, but I do like to browse, without using my hands if possible, and often encourage others to do so too!

Browsing Lime (*Tilia europea*) leaves

I like to get down on hands and knees to browse cleaver tips, violet leaves, violet flowers, red dead nettles, navelwort, wild garlic, primrose flowers and leaves...I know this might seem a bit crackers, but I really enjoy it! Give it a go. Being right down at herb level you can smell the plants you are eating, and as you eat, you get to look closely at the forms and colours around you. You find out where each plant likes living, who its mates are and see other tasty morsels nearby... it is very easy to get absorbed, into the moment and not hear the hoard of ramblers in rustling raingear coming over the brow of the hill...

If you do care what people might think about this kind of behaviour then it's just as satisfying to remain standing and browse from the trees. If someone does happen to wander along at this point you can always pretend you are studying something closely on a twig in front of you if you like. Hawthorn leaves are one of the first edible tree leaves to unfurl...so let out your inner deer and get browsing. If browsing is a bit much then simply hand pick a range of spring edibles and pop them in a bowl to make a beautiful salad. Add a simple dressing if the fancy takes you. If you time the picking right, the baked potato you put in the embers, or the oven, before you went out foraging will be ready when you get back!

A delicious salad with spring greens, (hairy bitter cress, hawthorne leaves, ground ivy leaves, violet flowers, cleaver tips, gorse flowers and stitchwort) mixed into a traditional green salad with olives. Mmmmm!

Learning about wild edible plants and hedge medicine is what got me started on the 'bushcraft' path. At college, I lived with a guy who knew about herbal medicine. He was amazing, and had a simple home remedy for almost anything. He would fix our hangovers with a mug of ginger tea. We would forage for ramsons in spring, and go out looking for ground ivy and coltsfoot to make into a lung tonic for winter coughs. But what I remember most was being introduced to nettles, and the soups and curries we would make with numb fingers.

Nettles are one of my best plant friends during springtime. By the time of the call of the first chiff-chaff, nettle tips are already out of the ground, enjoying warm rays from a sun climbing higher into the sky every day. Picking nettles without getting stung is a bit of an art, but easily mastered with a little practice. I eat loads. My wife and I pick nettle tips by the basket full. We dry them slowly in the airing cupboard for tea throughout the year. I have been drinking nettle tea religiously during the winter for many years. It is a great blood cleanser and full of calcium and iron and vitamins. Not only is it good medicine for me, but also for the planet, as the nettles have travelled less than a mile to get to my lips!

A Nettle tip (*Urtica dioica*) in spring.

One winter, I made a new blend of tea; nettle, elderflower and hibiscus flowers. Yum! The nettles (come) came from a copse 100 yards away from my house, and the elderflowers came from a favourite old 'grandmother tree' down the lane. Elderflowers have many medicinal qualities and helping the body fight against coughs, colds and flu. The hibiscus is rich in vitamin C. Fantastic I thought. But the hibiscus flowers came from a trip my wife made to Mexico. I started down the slippery slope of thinking about food miles again and how much pollution is caused by my early morning brew...

Most of us have heard about the concept of 'food miles' - the amount of miles our food travels to get to our plates or mugs and ultimately our mouths. I come from a generation very used to getting any kind of fruit or vegetable I want at any time of year. Apples come from as far as Chile and New Zealand to get to our supermarket shelves, with a large hidden cost that you and I, and all our relations in the web of life have to pay for.

How? It is difficult to see immediately as so much of our food is grown elsewhere. We don't generally experience the destruction of habitats and landscapes where the bulk of the crops are grown- the loss of soil quality, and the ground-water pollution from the growing process. We don't always get to see the air pollution from making and running the planes, trains, ships and trucks that transport our food. We are not informed of the human cost to the communities displaced by, or involved in, the growing, harvesting and processing. We are paying the price for the cost of industrial scale food production, not with our wallets, but with the loss of biodiversity, wild places, air and water quality.

I am no saint and, for example, still buy a lot of tomatoes from 'poly tunnel land' in Southern Spain during the winter months. However, nowadays I am increasingly aware of the wider costs of this way of eating and that's why as a family we have joined a local veg box scheme. We get seasonal veg that is organically grown less than 10 miles away. It's a small step to reducing food miles but we take further small steps by supporting other local producers as much as we can, and it tastes so much nicer! The ultimate is to be self-reliant as a community and grow all the vegetables we need within a few miles of home. We are a few years off that dream...yet, to borrow a phrase from a supermarket I avoid as much as possible, 'every little helps!'

Foraging is a great way to get us thinking about contemporary living and the effects of getting our food from where it grows to our lips. When we forage along hedgerows we really are eating locally produced food. By browsing, we get enzymes and vitamins in an unaltered state. No energy goes into cooking and thus altering some of the nutrients. I am not saying eat raw from the bushes every day. I am saying do it some of the time, and reduce the global footprint of your eating habits. Let us unite as 'bushcrafty' people and eat local produce for the greater good of all!

Yes, even thistles are edible if you know how.

However, it's not possible for all of us in the UK to go out and forage for the food we need; I don't think there is enough to go around for a start. England would look like a plague of locusts had just popped by for tea! That brings me neatly to caretaking, leaving enough for the other creatures whose lives depend on local resources to survive. No matter how we satisfy our daily nutritional needs, we are always affecting the lives of other organisms, when we forage the impacts become visible much closer to home. So let's have respect and gratitude. Let's take care, to leave enough for the plant to regenerate itself, and leave something for other folks to eat. Let's pick in a way that doesn't harm the plant too much...why dig up a violet, when you can pick off a few leaves for your salad, and pop them into a bowl with a little song of "thank you"?

So, how do you find out what to pick and what not? I had a lucky start, and have continued by looking in books. There are many books on the market, *Food for Free* by Richard Mabey being one of the best known. Each forager will probably have their favourite...at the moment I am trying out a few new delights from *Food from the Wild* by Ian Burrows, and there is a great website called *eatweeds.co.uk* that has clear instructions on how to gather and prepare many English plants However, in the tradition of passing things on orally, with whole body (and taste bud) learning, the best way to find out what is edible and what is not is to go out with someone who knows.

If you want to find out about farmers markets try The National Association of Farmers Markets, 0845 45 88 420 www.farmersmarkets.net. As for vegetable boxes/bag schemes, I am sure your local health food shop would be a good place to start. Happy foraging!

Partly chopped cow parsley (*Anthriscus sylvestris*), picked before flowering – excellent with butter and new potatoes, but not to be confused with deadly hemlock (*Conium maculatum*).

Fairy Plates
**Ages 4 and up,
Groups size: up
to 16
30-60 mins**

Ready

This activity provides a simple framework for gathering, identifying and learning about plants. You may want to focus the learning on edibility, or broaden the learning to other uses, such as symmetry, leaf margin types or flower shapes.

The basic idea is to gather a number of different leaves, flowers, fruit and possibly roots and seeds too. These are then arranged in a beautiful way, and laid out as offerings for the Fairies (not for us to eat!). Fairies love beautiful offerings from us humans, especially when the offerings are saying *thank you* to the nature spirits. Some say fairies love honey and songs most, yet others say they like our love and attention best.

In groups, we gather up some leaves, flowers and roots, lay them out beautifully on a large leaf plate, and place them somewhere we think the fairies would like to accept our offerings. When we are all ready, we visit each fairy plate to find out which plants we humans could eat, if we wanted to. Remember to leave enough flowers and leaves on the plants for all the bees, butterflies and caterpillars too!

Get set

You can use normal or paper plates, however, to be more natural and create an offering that doesn't need to be disturbed, use a large leaf, a circle of leaves, some string in a circle or even make a plate shaped clearing in the leaves or sand.

If you do not have the knowledge in your head you will also need a reliable field guide for identifying the plants and perhaps also a book that tells you what is edible.

Check your chosen gathering area for plants known to cause rashes or skin eruptions...I am thinking mostly of Giant Hogweed here, but also nettles.

Go!

"Who believes in elves and fairies?

"Did you know that fairies like pretty offerings from us humans?

"Did you know they like little snacks and honey?

"Let's make some little fairy plates, with some of the leaves and flowers we think the fairies would like!"

With the students working as individuals, pairs or small groups, hand out some large dock leaves, butterbur or heliotrope leaves, all of which are safe to touch, for the groups to use as plates. Either that, or show them where to pick their own leaf plate or how to make a plate with a circle of sticks or stones on the ground.

When everyone is ready with their own plates, we go off to collect beautiful and potentially tasty items for the offering.

"Ooh! I bet the fairies like these", I say, looking at some pretty leaves, and so I take a few, singing "thank you!" to the plant as I do so. Usually the group disperses and individuals collect their own chosen things to put on the plates. I start to arrange the foliage and flowers in a way I find appealing and artistic.

After about ten minutes check in with the groups to see how much longer they need, and round up the activity. Visit each offering plate in turn, verbally acknowledging the care, love and attention that went into the offerings to boost the children's artistic self esteem as much as possible.

I like to ask if anyone knows the names of the plants on the plate to see what the group knows before telling people about the plants. We identify and name the plants, pointing out key features particular to the plant – perhaps it has a square stem, with leaves that come off the stem in pairs, or small, trumpet-shaped flowers, that sort of thing, keeping it fairly simple.

If possible, let people know whether the plant is edible, harmless or poisonous to humans. Other information can also be shared if known, like medicinal uses, folklore and practical traditional uses. In ecology, the study of the interaction of life, plants and animals are organised in families. Which family a plant is in usually depends on the kinds of flowers they have. As we go from fairy plate to fairy plate there will be repetitions of the collected plants and it can be put to the group to remember what the plant is, whether it is edible and so on. When we have finished visiting the offerings they can be left for the fairies.

Spokes of a Wheel – a Collecting and Map Making Activity
Ages 7 and up
Group size: up to 16
Time about 30-45 mins

A 'tribe' making a map.

Ready
The plan is to form a circular map of the area around the wheel-like sculpture, which is made while doing the activity. This 'resource map' can speed up the process of finding out what's around, encourages everybody to look at their surroundings thoroughly, builds team spirit and can be a really enjoyable way to learn about the medicinal, edible and practical uses of plants. Grown-ups really get into the heady information element the wheel offers, while children like the colours and patterns that develop.

Get set
You will need to find a flat place where you can make a circle about 3-6ft across, on some kind of uniform surface. In the photo above, we used a large tree stump. You could also make the map on an area of sand, or bare earth.

Go!

"Come on in everyone!"

"Right, for this next activity, we need to collect a couple of straight sticks, up to 3ft long."

When the participants have brought back two sticks, we stand in a circle, facing inwards.

"Let's divide up the circle with the sticks, to form spokes and the rim of a wheel."

Once the spokes are in place, we stand up and shuffle around, so that each person gets a portion of the wheel, or cake, in front of them.

"Ok, let's turn around, face out from the wheel and walk away, in a straight line, picking up resources as we go...perhaps a leaf or two if there is a good pile of leaves for shelter building, a flower from a plant we want to know about or a sign left by an animal.

"We don't need anything large, just a little reminder. Keep checking over your shoulder to make sure that you're walking in a straight line!"

Imagine you are walking away from such a circle now, and you come to a pine tree and find a load of cones for getting the fire going in the morning, and so pick one of them up. Next, you come to a patch of sun dried, bleached grass just great for tinder so you grab a bit of that too. And then there's a cherry tree with a load of cherries still on it, so you also pick up a few of them. Oh, and there are some Lords and Ladies, a rather poisonous member of the lily family that you think the group ought to know about, so you pick a piece of that too. When your hands are full, usually after you have picked up five or so different resources, you turn around and return to the circle/wheel. As you lay them out in the order you found them, starting in the middle of the wheel working out towards the rim, you can't help but notice some of the other interesting things being laid out.

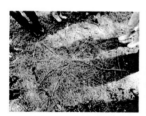  

When everybody is back and has placed their findings in the wheel...Hey presto! There's a sculpture that lets you know how near and how far certain resources are, and in which direction.

As facilitator, always ask people to share what they know about the resources in the circular map, as well as sharing what you know. The discussion draws in and involves the circle of people to an extent where all kinds of other topics pop up. It is almost magic, as this quote from a forest school leader in Devon explains:

"I've done this so many times since you first showed me and some of the stuff that comes out in the chat around the wheel is amazing. Lots of the kids' own risk assessments and rules / guidelines for our camps were decided (on) around the map wheel. Thanks!"

When people begin to lose interest, or the activity is finished, there is one more thing to say before we move on:

"If you find anything else interesting while we are out here, you can add it to the map for everyone to see!"

Comfrey Fritters!
All ages.
Up to 7-8 people per facilitator/cook
1 hour

Ready
Comfrey (*Symphytum officianale*) fritters are a very tasty snack that can be made easily on the wayside during the spring and early summer months, and are something that children usually enjoy. They can be made from many different kinds of batters, so can suit many varied dietary requirements. They are best accompanied by simple flavours, like salt, soy sauce, honey, lemon juice or maple syrup. (If you want to get fancy, you can add all kinds of flavouring to the batters like chopped herbs, spices or even curry paste.)

The activity is facilitator intensive, as one person can only cater for a small group of up to 7-8 people and the cooking is hot and busy. For bigger groups you may need a ratio of 1 cook per 6-10 munchers!

Get set
The batter is best mixed in advance for less 'faffing' at cooking time, especially with an eager bunch of children. For a simple vegan batter use chick-pea flour and water or soy milk and mix it into the consistency of pancake or Yorkshire pudding mix.

The kit you need will be something like: frying pan or wok, fire lighting kit, vegetable oil, fish slice or wayside chopsticks, leak proof container with ready mixed batter, (big enough to dunk the leaves in), soy sauce (or salt etc). You will need somewhere to light a small fire, preferably close to a patch of comfrey.

Optional extras might be paper towels or serviettes, silver service, wine, wine cooler...seriously, why not make an afternoon of it!

Go!

Collect young comfrey leaves, no longer than about 20cm long, because they tend to get a bit stringy the longer and older they are. Check them for bugs to keep the vegetarians, the bugs and the squeamish happy. Establish fireside rules. Get the fire going. Heat a 3-4cm depth of oil in the frying pan until a drop of batter will sizzle in the oil, dunk a leaf in the batter, place it in the pan (watch out for splatters of hot oil) and remove when the batter is golden. Allow to cool for a moment, before sprinkling with a little soy sauce, salt or syrup. Munch while hot!

Comfrey   All the kit ready to go...   Sizzle sizzle!

Only eat a few as they are very oily, and according to some research, eating handfuls a day of comfrey over a prolonged period could damage your liver or cause increased cancer growth. When Frank Cook, a plant enthusiast and forager of worldwide repute, was about this and he said:

"Basically, as foragers, we eat a far greater variety of edible plants than a supermarket consumer, and comfrey is just a small part of our nutritional mix. In small amounts I personally have no problem eating it. My biggest beef with the so-called research (on comfrey toxicity) is that the rats where fed huge amounts compared to their body weight. It goes back to that supermarket mindset, 'eat a lot of a little', whereas foragers 'eat a little of a lot'.

I continue to eat comfrey fritters, along with a huge variety of wild seasonal plants every spring with no apparent side effects. If you have any concerns try white dead nettle tips – they are a good substitute.

Spring Greens Stir-Fry
All ages
Group size: 6-8 people per cook
45 mins - 1 hour

Ready
Another very successful, wayside snack (in term of getting a positive response to eating wild food) is a simple stir-fry of freshly collected spring greens.

Get set
All you need for this is a little knowledge of what you can and cannot eat, a carrier bag or basket to collect the greens in, some vegetable oil, soy sauce, a wok, a fire to cook it all up on, perhaps a couple of pairs of secateurs, and a few willow, sycamore or hazel wands with which to make chopsticks. If your group is too young or unable to use chopsticks, use forks. If you want to be more 'native' in flavouring the stir-fry, then you could collect, dry and grind up some edible seaweeds to use as seasoning. Other alternatives are chopped up water pepper (*Persicaria hydropiper*), or perhaps some shop bought herb salt.

Wild Garlic or Ramsons (*Alium ursinum*) and Cleavers (*Galium saxatile*)

Go!

"Lets go for a wander and collect some tasty spring green. Look for nettle tips, chickweed, stitchwort, violet leaves, young birch, hawthorne and beech leaves, gorse flowers, vetch leaves and flowers, dandelion leaves, wild garlic... "

When we have collected about a carrier bag full of greens, which is a good quantity for 6-8 people, find a place suitable for a quick fire, or return to camp and use a fireplace there.

"Let's collect tinder and sticks and get the fire going".

While the oil heats up, I ask the group to make themselves some chopsticks. A pair of secateurs may be useful at this point. The ends of the chopsticks can be sterilised in the flames or the bark can be scraped off. If the group isn't old enough to make their own ask one of the adults present to make the chopsticks. Check through the greens to make sure everything is edible. When the oil is hot, toss in the greens, stir them round, add a little water to aid the steaming and finally add some seasoning. Once all the nettles are wilted the stinging hairs no longer sting, so they can safely be eaten. It's now ready. Hey presto! Enjoy the snack, full of vitamins, minerals and chlorophyll, munching directly from the wok, with your chopsticks.

Stitchwort (*Stellaria holostea*) flowers and tips make a delicious addition to a spring greens stir fry.

Chapter 3

It's Sharp.

Sharpening up

In this chapter we look at some of the techniques of safely using three tools commonly used in the 'bushcrafty' world, namely the fixed blade knife, the pruning saw, and the small axe. I will also employ a couple of other tools briefly; the Japanese rasp and the hook knife.

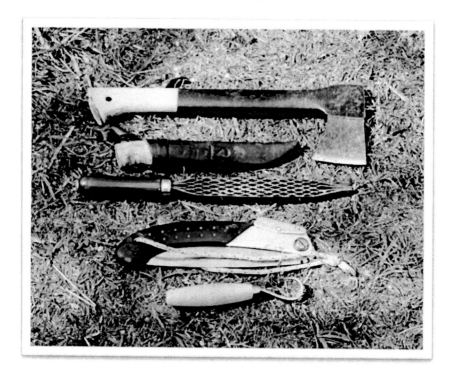

Learning how to use a tool by reading a book will not suit all people, (including myself!) but hopefully the activities demonstrated here with lots of photos will help you along the way to feeling confident in using these tools. As the old saying goes 'a picture says a thousand words' - so look at the pictures carefully.

Useful things to know

It seems obvious, but I must say it; while learning to use sharp tools, encourage people to cut away from their bodies. There are some more advanced ways of using a fixed blade knife that involve moving the blade towards the body, but I will not go into these in this book.

As a general rule, I do not start teaching knife use until the students are at least 7 years old. This is not only because of the attention the facilitator must give to younger students, but also the student needs to be large enough and strong enough to handle the tools safely. I do teach tool use to younger people, but only on a one to one basis.

Keep your blades as sharp and clean as possible to minimise the effort required to use the tool. A blunt tool is more dangerous, as more force has to be used to make it cut, and it is less likely to cut in precisely the way you direct it.

Of course, accidents do happen, so keep the mind positive and first aid kit handy.

Work for short periods of time to maintain focus, an hour at a time is the maximum; longer tasks should be split up into separate sessions.

A dull or tired mind is not suited to working with sharp tools. If I think my students are a bit dozy, and we are about to do work with sharp tools, I will do some kind of quick, aerobic activity to wake up their brain cells, and encourage both sides of their brains to be involved in the activity. A set of star jumps, for example, a bit of running on the spot, some kind of 'cross-crawling' and a few 'breaths of eternal focus' should do the trick. You may want to develop your own routine, but in case you want to know more about cross crawling and breaths of eternal focus here is a little explanation.

'**Cross-crawling**' is a term for mind-body exercises in which one part of the right hand side of the body, crosses in-front of the eyes, to touch a part of the left hand side of the body, and vice versa. Cross-crawling is *said* (not conclusively proved) to facilitate balanced nerve activation across the *corpus callosum* (that part in your brain that connects the right half to the left half.) When done on a regular basis, more nerve networks form and more connections are made in the *corpus callosum*, thus making communication between the two hemispheres faster and more integrated.

The **Cross-crawl** is simply a 'cross-lateral walking in place exercise'. By touching the right elbow to the left knee and then the left elbow to the right knee, large areas of both brain hemispheres are activated at the same time. Why not stand up and have a go now?!

The **breath of eternal focus** is a breathing exercise to focus the mind and still the hands. I came up with the name after watching Kung Fu Panda, usually said with a twinkle in the eye and a kung fu instructor's accent! To do a breath of eternal focus, stand with your feet shoulder-width apart and knees slightly bent. Your hands will naturally rest on the top of your thighs. As you slowly breathe in through your nose (if possible), raise your hands, palms down, until they are roughly the same height as your mouth. Then, breathing out, with a 'tssssss' sound (if you wish!), pretend you are drawing a bow to one side of your body, by extending your arm, palm facing forward, until it is straight. At the same time, pretend you are pulling a bowstring to your ear, with your other hand. Keep your eyes focused on the index finger of your 'bow hand' as it moves away from your face. There should be no strain to the bow drawing movements, yet I find it most effective if I imagine there is some kind of resistance in the air, as if it were thick mud. When the out breath is finished let your hands relax and arc down to a resting position in-front of the top of your thighs, before starting the breath again. Repeat several times.

The fixed blade knife

Using knives in groups can be worrisome for many people. However, I know of no other activity that brings such stillness, focus and close attention to detail for both the leader and the students! I think that this kind of craftwork changes the brainwaves of the students. A kind of peace descends and the wildlife comes back into camp. The less worries you have as a leader the fewer the chances are that the students may fulfil your unspoken fears.

It is equally important to know how to pass and receive a knife safely. Passing a sharp tool to someone needs some degree of trust, and I find it useful to insist on eye contact when people are passing tools to each other, to develop that trust.

In order to do all of the above I hold a 'circle of trust.'

The circle of trust
Ages 8 and over
Group size: up to 20

Ready
It is worth spending some time developing the feeling of trust between the people in your group. When teaching the use of sharp tools I like to set up a 'circle of trust', through the process of learning to pass the tool (a knife in the case outlined below), safely from one person to another. When people in a group trust one another, they are more likely to work together, and respond to guidance, making the job of the facilitator much easier.

Get set
Gather everyone in a circle. You will need one of the knives you are using for the whittling and craft activities.

Go!
"I want to introduce you to the tool we are going to be using. It is a fixed blade knife. Let's sit down for a few minutes."

Taking the knife out from its sheath, talk about the features of the knife for a minute or two before saying,

"It is useful to know how to pass a knife to someone else, for your own safety and theirs. This way of passing a knife is the safest (see the picture below). The knife is held in the hand, between the thumb and forefinger. The sharp part of the blade is facing upwards and away from the back of the wrist. The handle is pointing towards the person you are passing the knife to."

Looking at the person next to me in the circle I say:

"As I reach out to pass the knife, I get eye contact with that person and say, 'Hello. This is a knife.' I then pass them the knife, handle first, like this."

That person receives the knife, positions the knife in their hands so it's ready to be passed on, establishes eye contact with the next person and says, "Hello. This is a knife," before passing it on, and so on, round the circle. When the knife gets back, send it round the circle the other way, sheathing the knife when it gets returns, and move on to the next activity.

This is the way I teach people to pass a knife.

Getting Familiar with a Knife as a Tool
Ages 8 and over
Group: up to 16
15 mins

Ready
A fixed blade knife is basically a metal blade, with some part of the blade made into a handle, and another part sharpened to form a cutting edge. This kind of knife is safer than a penknife because they are stronger and have no folding mechanism.

It is important to be used to handling a tool; feeling its weight and balance in our hands, taking it safely out and returning it equally safely to its cover or sheath, and holding it comfortably, in readiness for work.

Working with a sharp edged tool needs boundaries. I use the concept of the 'blood bubble' to define initial safe working areas. A blood bubble is the area in which blood could be drawn, if someone were to enter it, and the tool were being used without enough awareness. Initially I make sure all sharp tool users keep to their own blood bubble, one that is the size of their outstretched arms. When skill and awareness levels increase the blood bubble size gets smaller, and tool users can begin to work closer together. It is worthwhile creating a whittling area, so that when the students are not under instruction, they have a chance to use tools in a more independent and less supervised way, but somewhere where eyes can be keep an eye on them. A thick piece of rope laid on the ground is perfect for this job, but many other things will do to define an area for this purpose.

Get set
You will need a knife for each person, and somewhere to sit on the ground in a circle - a circle of cut rounds of wood or logs that are stable to sit on would also be fine.

Go!
"Okay everybody, come and sit down in a knee-to-knee circle, I want to do a tool safety talk before we use the tools."

When we are sitting down, and attentive, I hold up one of the fixed blade knives we are going to use.

"This is the tool we are going to use. It is a fixed blade knife. It is safer to use than a penknife because there is no chance of the blade folding over and cutting your fingers. At the moment it is in its sheath. Taking it in and out of the sheath safely requires technique and practice. We will all have some practice shortly."

Taking the knife out of the sheath, while demonstrating how to do so safely, i.e. holding the knife steady while moving the sheath away from the knife blade, point out it has a razor sharp edge on one side of the blade and show how to test if a blade is sharp enough to work with. This can be done in two ways. One is by resting the blade on a thumb-nail, perpendicular to it, using only the weight of the blade as a downward force, and seeing if it bites or scrapes into the nail as the blade is pushed away gently. It does? It's sharp. The other is to look along the blade edge to see if there is any light bouncing of the blade where the two honed edges meet – no light? It's sharp.

When the knife is back in its sheath, it's time to talk about 'blood bubbles'.

"A blood bubble is a safe working space you make for yourself by stretching out your arms and making sure they don't touch or enter anyone else's blood bubble. Everybody get into your own blood bubbles please, with a log to sit on and work at."

When everyone is settled the knives can be handed out.

"You will now be given the chance to get familiar with the tools you are going to use. Keep the knives in their sheaths until I have given the instruction to take them out."

When ready the instruction can be given. After a few minutes of practice, the instruction is given to sheath knives. When all the knives are away they are placed the on the stump. We all leave the work area for a five-minute break!

Splitz-Kids
7 and up
Group size: up to 16 (for 2-3 facilitators)
Time 45 mins-1hr

Ready
Once familiar with a fixed blade knife, I like to teach a set of basic knife use techniques through the process of making a "splitz-kid" The end result is a small throwing stick that can be used for the game of "splitz".

Get set
Each person will need a knife and a piece of straight grained, little finger thick, green wood, about 60cm long. A willow or hazel wand would do nicely.

Arrange the group so they are in their own 'blood bubbles'. Each person could also have a log to sit on.

Go!
First of all, give a demonstration of how to make a splitz-kid, using the following cuts:

The knee cut

Sit or kneel steadily on a log or the ground, bending one of your legs so the thigh is 90 degrees or more to the shin. Holding the handle of the knife in your favoured hand, place the back of the knife blade just under the kneecap, so it rests in the little depression there. The knife should not move! It is braced against the knee. The stick you are working on is drawn underneath the blade towards the person, to one side of the body. There are two basic positions. It doesn't matter which hand you use the knife in. You can either be **same hand, same knee** or **hand to opposite knee**! Check out the picture! Using the part of the blade closest to the handle, sharpen the fatter end (the butt) of the stick to a sharp point.

Whittling to the side

The hand holding the stick goes across the body and rests on the opposite thigh, so that the hand holding the knife can work to the outside of the thigh, cutting down and out. This time the knife moves, not the stick, to take off the ridges between the cuts made during the first step. Again, use the part of the blade closest to the handle of the knife.

Elbows on the knees cut

For this cut, the elbows are placed on the knees – to keep the sharp pointy blade away from the arteries in the inner thigh. With the elbows on the knees, both hands can be brought up in front of the eyes – not too close, obviously! – so that close attention can be brought to the work. The knife moves, the stick is held steady. Usually the part of the blade used is the part closest to the handle, though the part nearer the tip can be used too. Holding knife and stick like this means you can remove the smaller ridges remaining from whittling to your side.

Thumb push

In the same position as the 'elbows on the knee' cut, or as in this picture with elbows near the waist, any part of the blade, including the area near the tip, is used to take very fine shavings off the point of the stick being sharpened, until it looks almost like a sharpened pencil. The thumb pushes the back of the knife blade, giving control and strength to the cut, albeit over a short distance.

Scraping

The final method is to turn the blade at right angles to the point of the stick and to scrape away any ridges left until there is a perfectly round point to the stick. Scraping can be done with elbows on the knees, elbows by the waist or working to the side (as this photo shows).

The rosette cut

The rosette cut is used when we want to cut through a stick, sometimes in a precise place, but don't have the strength to get through the wood with the knee cut, or we don't have a saw. We could utilise this method to shorten the stick, for example. Hold the un-worked end of the stick, pointing upwards. Whittling to the side or using the thumb push cut, using the part of the blade closest to the handle. After each cut spin the stick in your hand slightly, make another cut, then repeat until the stick 'breaks' in two or the two halves can be twisted apart. (The following photos show the rosette cut being done to the side, to illustrate the point, not as part of the process of making a splitz kid. To see a splitz-kid with a hairdo see the first picture in the series of a Jodie holding the one she made towards the camera.)

We now have a stick with a point and a hair-do! Add facial features, like eyes, eyelashes, nose and mouth to further practise the thumb push cut and the 'always cut away' from the body rule (to see a splitz-kid with a hair-do see the first picture in this section of Jodie proudly holding up the on she made towards the camera).

Playing Splitz!

As a child of nine I used to play this game with a friend, on the lawn. As we got older we progressed (?!) from sticks to sharp pointy knives in the dark. I do still have all my toes in case you are asking! Make sure all players are wearing shoes, preferably something thicker than wellies, just in case.

To play, the pair of contestants face each other, about a pace apart with their feet together to begin with. The aim is to make your opponents do the splitz or fall over because their feet are too far apart to keep balanced. The contestants take it in turns to throw their splitz-kid, so that it sticks, pointy end into the ground, on one side or the other of their opponent's feet. If, for example, George is successful in getting his stick into the ground, then Sam has to move his nearest foot until it touches George's stick, without moving his other foot. Sam then passes George back his stick. It's now Sam's turn to throw his stick into the ground...

Making tongs
10 mins per tong

A sycamore bowl being made using tongs (made from sweet chestnut) and hot coals.

Ready
Tongs are very useful tools to have around the fire for tasks like picking up bits of burning wood that have rolled out of the fire, re-arranging the logs and picking up embers for bowl burning. They are also relatively simple to make and the process takes us from harvesting the wood to the finished product in a couple of simple steps.

Pruning
There is an art to pruning a branch off a tree – it's very easy to leave a nasty scar on the tree if you are not sure what you are doing. A cleaner, smoother cut will heal more quickly and is less likely to cause rot or lead to infection in the tree. A 'stop-cut' can be employed, to the

underside (of the branch being cut), before cutting a branch off a trunk, to stop the bark tearing off down the tree as the limb is cut. The job is finished with a third cut nearer the collar, or shoulder (the slightly raised bit the branch grows out of on the trunk).

Now you see it.

Three cuts later, now you don't!

This cut is too close to the trunk.

Ouch! No stop cut causes tearing.

Coppicing

Some trees, like ash, chestnut, hazel, and willow produce many straight stems from the base of the trunk, especially when coppiced. Coppicing is a traditional method of woodland management in which young tree stems are cut down to near ground level. New shoots will then emerge from the base of the 'stool', which can be harvested again and again. Depending on the tree and the kinds of resources needed the coppicing cycles will vary from 1 year to more than 12. Coppicing effectively keeps the coppiced tree at a young stage in its growth pattern, and so it can end up living much longer than a single stemmed tree – there's a 2000-year-old lime tree at Westonbirt Arboretum, for example. There will be more about coppicing and its relevance to sustainable living in Chapter 7.

Folding Saws

Folding saws are an increasingly common addition to the camper and bushcrafter rucksack. With appropriate instruction, they are also quite suitable for use in forest schools. A well-designed pruning saw leaves a clean, smooth cut, and I recommend versions that require a pulling action to cut through the wood. A folding saw will often leave a cleaner cut than a bow saw, get into smaller places, and is easier to slip into your pocket and transport safely. I prefer to use the type of folding saw that is used by tree surgeons because the blades are strong and sharp, with teeth angled to work with minimum effort and to leave the smoothest cut. When possible it is safest to place the arm and hand holding the branch to be cut over the one handling the saw – so that if the saw blade comes out of the cut, it doesn't go onto the hand holding the branch.

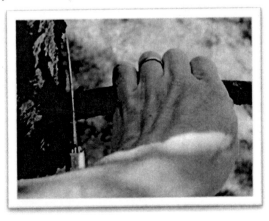

To make the tongs!

Depending on what kind of wood you have there are different ways of making tongs. The photos that follow show a technique where a stem or branch is split down the middle, using a fixed blade knife.

Collect some straight-grained wood, preferably with a knot or a fork at one end, about 50-60cm long and 2-3cm thick. If it's thinner than 2cm, it is likely to bend as you are trying to split, or cleave it.

Place the stick, knot end down, on a hard surface like a tree stump. Make an initial split in the wood using a fixed blade knife and a baton – you may need to work in pairs to get the first 15cm of wood cleaved. Twisting the knife blade in the cut can also help. When you can get your fingers and thumbs on the two sides of the wood you can then work the wood in your hands to split it further by gently pulling the two sides apart. Try to keep the split running down the centre of the wood. If the split runs off to one side you can try to get the split to return to the middle by bending the thicker of the two split pieces more acutely as you pull the two pieces apart. Take a look at the pictures (sorry they are a bit busy!). If you need to apply more force, as on a thicker piece of wood, you can use your knee on a stump rather than your thumbs.

When the wood is split to a suitable length (or when you get to the knot), find a twig to wedge in the split to hold the two sides of the tongs apart. And there you have some useable tongs.

If you are making the tongs in spring, from willow for example, the bark comes off very easily, and if you peel off the willow bark in strips, you can use it as cordage to bind in the twig wedge for longer lasting tongs.

Using a Small Axe and Fire to make a Bowl.
Ages 12 and over
Group size: up to 8 per facilitator
6 hours

They *are* burning bowls, not smoking huge cigars, honest!

Ready

This activity is suitable for people who can wield an axe. By wield, I don't mean run into battle twirling one round your head, I mean having the strength in the arm to pick one up and use it safely to chop. You will know if you can, and if those in your care can. When working with younger folks the leader can always prepare the bowls in advance, so the youngsters can do the bowl-burning bit. If you are doing the preparation, watch out for repetitive strain on the forearms, if you are not used to using an axe often! I shall write this section as if I am teaching an individual to make the bowl, rather than as if I were teaching a whole group.

Get set

Seasoned sycamore logs 12-15 cm in diameter are ideal for this. Alternative woods include ash (which can also be used unseasoned), hawthorne, apple, pear, cherry, maple and beech. We will need a saw, an axe and a baton or mallet to make the bowl. For finishing the bowl you can use a japanese rasp and a hook knife. You will also need an established fire with lots of embers and perhaps some elder stems to make straws to blow through. A straw helps focus the air stream and, if it's the right bore, it extends the time breathed out per breath. Sections of elder about 5-7cm long by 2-3 cm thick are just about right for the job, with the pith pushed out with a piece of fence wire or a 10cm nail.

Go!
Cutting a bowl blank
To cut a bowl blank, we will need a log in the round, about 15 cm in diameter. It is best if the wood has been seasoned for at least few months first. Using a saw cut a piece about 20 cm long, 25 -30cm if you want to have a handle on the bowl.

Split the wood in half lengthways. This can be done with a well aimed shot (eyes left!), or by placing the blade of the axe on one end of the blank, holding the end of the axe handle and giving the poll (the back of the axe head) a good whack with a baton or mallet.

Choose one half of the wood. Rest the blank on a tree stump, or sturdy log.

Sliding your hand up the axe handle to rest comfortably near the head, use the axe with more control, to make a start at the 'bowl' of the bowl. Move the blank around so you are free to chop, in a vertical plane, into the wood at all angles, whilst always keeping the bowl blank between your body and the axe head.

Burning the bowl
When enough of a depression has been created for some hot coals from the fire to sit in, put the axe away safely and pick up the tongs.

To be very health and safety conscious, we wear safety goggles, put the bowls on the ground and then lie down on our bellies to blow on the embers in the bowl.

Pick out a coal about the size of a cherry tomato and place it into the depression. Blow on the coal, concentrating the stream of air where the coal comes into contact with the wood, using long, steady breaths. When the bowl is at face level, most of the rising smoke and sparks go on up past the face. As the coal burns down into the depression, there may be flames and the bowl may get very hot. Slowly, surely, the bowl depression gets bigger. This task teaches patience and persistence.

Loaded up ready to blow coals

Using an elder straw to blow on the

Be sure to leave a rim. Bowls can be left out in the wind during the depression burning process, so we don't have to blow on them as often, and they can even be left for hours at a time to go cold, to be continued later. The bowl-burning process can be stopped rapidly, in parts or all of the depression, by adding a handful of earth or sand, or pouring on water.

Cleaning out the inside of the bowl.
The inside can be scraped out using sticks, sharp stones or even a metal spoon. To get a better finish to the inside of the bowl, a hook-knife can be

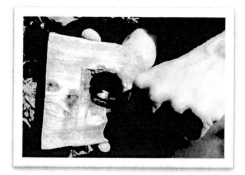

used by adults, or those students most controlled and proficient at whittling. The inside can then be sealed with some olive oil.

Shaping the outside

The outside of the bowl can be shaped, again using a chopping action with the axe, or, more suitable for younger arms, a Japanese rasp – safe to use and incredibly effective.

Making a handle

To make a handle for the bowl, 'stop cuts' can be used to help split off the wood surrounding the part that's to be your handle, without splitting the bowl in half. 'Stop cuts' stop wood from splitting or tearing along the grain at the point of the cut. However, a misplaced stop-cut or axe cut can result in tears as the bowl splits in two. GO CAREFULLY! Look at how the grain moves along the wood. Diagonal stop cuts, and cutting off the corners of the bowl, can save quite a bit of work during the shaping process.

Using a (ghostly!) baton to control the axe. Notice the diagonal cuts on the corners of the bowl.

Magic Wands
Ages 7 and up
Groups: up to 16 with two leaders
2 hrs or more

Ready
It seems that boys, given the chance, want to make spears. This may not be practical or safe. A shorter alternative is a wand. Wand making allows the maker to be creative with his or her newly developed whittling abilities and to play at being a wizard or witch. It also presents an opportunity for using natural glue, made from tree resin and charcoal, to set in a special stone or gem as decoration. I like wands to be about the same length as the persons' forearm or shorter, and up to the thickness of the base of the makers' thumb. I tend to use woods like hazel, oak, beech, pine, sycamore, holly, yew, bay, steering away from elder for respectful reasons! (It can be useful to know some of the lore associated with each of the trees, just in case your wand maker's want to know what their wand might be especially good for, so there are few books in the reference section for this purpose).

> **Some Elder Lore**
> Elder trees are sacred to the goddess Bride, and said to be a place where spirits of the dead dwell. Cutting down an Elder tree released them to haunt the unfortunate woodcutter, unless the correct song was sung, ritual performed or words muttered. If I need to take something from an Elder tree I will always say something like: "Grandma Elder. Thank you for you wood (flowers, berries...). You can have a piece of me when I die".

Get set
Wearing an item or two of appropriate costume clothing helps to get us all into the spirit of a planned activity, and this is no exception. A simple cloak will do, but a wizard hat might just complete the picture. You will also need a folding saw(s), a knife for everyone, fine grit sandpaper for finishing off, coniferous tree resin, a small quantity of beeswax perhaps, a tin can to warm the glue in, tongs or thick leather gloves to move the can in and out of the fire, incense and charcoal (I like the loose kind of incense, made from natural blended herbs, gums and resins, that is burnt on a charcoal disc, or a hot coal from the fire) or perhaps some dried sage, juniper, cedar or lavender (sticks, leaves or flowers will do. You might also want a few books on tree lore, in case your students are interested and like looking up that kind of information.

Go!
The prayer for the hunt
"In a moment we are going off wand 'hunting'"

"Not just any old piece of wood will do for a wand. The seeker of a wand needs to listen to the trees and feel guided towards a particular piece of wood. The spirits of the trees will be calling you to work for them, just as you are calling them to provide you with a wand. Hunters also give thanks for the animals they are about to hunt, before they go out, to ensure success and to ask the spirit of the land for a suitable quarry. Let's make up our own prayers to say in our heads, giving thanks for the wands we are about to receive."

At this point, light some nice woody incense like Tibetan Incense, or perhaps a smudge stick with cedar and juniper in it, explaining that Gods and Spirits like incense, and that it helps carry our prayers to them.

Hunting and making the wands
When ready, we set off to collect wands, with the leader staying out of the decision making process as much as possible, except if the piece of wood is too long or fat, so that the wand is genuinely personal to each wand maker.

Depending on the age and ability of the group, I will either assist the cutting of the chosen branches on a one-to-one basis, or send them off to gather wands themselves, reminding them to leave any wood they discard neatly at the base of the tree it came from. Once back at camp the shaping and decorating begins.

Making natural glue
The glue is used when someone wants to add a stone they have found to the tip or shaft of the wand. To make the glue, collect tree resin from conifer trees in a clean tin can using a knife or a stick. Hard blobs can often be knocked off with a sideways blow from a rock held in the hand. Warm the resin until liquid – carefully, because if it gets too hot it will burst into flames! Add a little powdered charcoal, beeswax or eggshell. Stir it in. Apply with a stick, or warmed metal applicator – a spoon handle is good. Leave to cool and set. This glue is not waterproof.

Wand purifying and dedication ceremony
When all the wands are finished, we gather round, so we can purify and dedicate wands in a ceremony. Smudging is a purification process using smoke to clear unwanted thoughts, feeling or spirits. We can use the smoke from a small fire made with dried sage, cedar, lavender or juniper sticks, alternatively or light some more incense.

"May all these wands be used for the greater good of all beings!"

One by one, I ask the wandmakers to pass their wands through the smoke. Then we gather in a close circle (away from the smoke!), and altogether, we point the tips of our wands to the sky, touching them together in the middle.

"All for One!"

We then all touch the butts of our wand handles to the ground (to always be connected with the earth) as we say,

"And One for all!

Making wishes

To finish off the ceremony and the activity we sit on the ground and think of one wish that we would like to make, that would make the world a better place for all the plants and creatures, including humans.

After a few moments, I invite people to say their wishes out loud, by saying them to say, " I wish..." and zapping the air with their wand.

As each person expresses their wish, add another tiny piece of incense to the charcoal, or a few more herds to the fire. When we have all said our wishes add a final pinch of incense and say,

"May all these wishes be granted!"

Chapter 3 & ¾

Pen - Mightier than the Sword!

"The pen is mightier than the sword" is an adage coined by Edward Bulwer-Lytton in 1839. A pen or pencil is a valuable tool – and so is a notebook. For years I have had a 'wossige' book. My wossige book is a hard-backed notebook, usually un-ruled, for writing things down in, taking bark and leaf rubbings, doing drawings in, and even chopping vegetables on when camping. I use it for writing poems, doing sketches, writing lists, remembering ideas and for processing feelings by emptying my whirling brain onto paper (something like a paper version of the 'pensieve' used by Professor Dumbledore in Harry Potter).

Not everybody likes to use pen and paper, but when any writing or drawing is treated light heartedly, with no pressure on how people want to express themselves, using a note book, or even making our own books from scrap paper and card, (like the ones made by Creeping Toad to the right), can be a lot of fun and results in a group of very proud people.

Seven Directions Poem – Poems from the Heart

To the East I see a lovely old church,
To the South I see a bridge,
To the West I see an enchanted wood,
To the North I see a path leading far away,
Above I see rain struck puffy clouds,
Below I see spring flowers on the ground
Inside I feel loved,
Altogether, I am happy.
I give thanks for all there is.

By Dotty, age 9

Ready

The seven directions poems are lovely and simple to do, especially written at sunrise, when the day is fresh, the birds are singing with open hearts and you know which direction you are facing in! Of course, you can do this activity at any other time of day, you just need to have *some* way of telling which way you are facing to start the poem off facing East.

In the process of drawing in inspiration for the poem, I ask the participants to send their attention to their hearts, and develop a heartfelt connection with the outside world, before we begin to write. Our hearts operate on many different levels. Stephen Harrod Buhner, a poet and a senior researcher for the Foundation of Gaian Studies, has this to say about the heart in his book *The Secret Teachings of Plants:*

> *"At its most basic, the heart is a pump, circulating blood and generating pressure waves throughout the body. But the heart, it turns out, is much more than a muscular pump (and there is some question to whether it is a muscular pump at all). It is an electromagnetic generator, producing a wide range of electromagnetic frequencies; an endocrine gland, making and releasing hormones; and a part of the central nervous system. It is, in fact, a brain in its own right. (The heart has)...deep impacts not only on our physiological functioning and health, but also on how we think and feel – in fact, on our consciousness."*

Get set

You will need a compass (kept hidden, so you can appear very wise by knowing which direction is East!), pens and card, or notebooks, to write in. Something to sit on, if the ground is wet or damp. Perhaps some colouring pencils, two or three per person.

Go!

"Gather in, everybody. Here is some card and a pencil to write a special poem with. Let's sit down in a huddle, all facing the rising sun (or simply the East), with enough room for every person to shuffle round in a circle, on the spot." We have a bit of fun and a wriggle getting into the best position.

Turning to face everyone, I say "We are about to write a poem, using all our senses. Please write these three words at the top of you page:

"To the East,"

I centre myself in the here and now, and invite everyone else to do the same by having few deep breaths, with their eyes closed.

94

"Without telling me, and keeping your eyes closed, can you smell anything? Can you feel the air going down into your lungs? Can you feel, or hear your heart beating? Imagine warm, soft rays, like sunshine, coming out from your heart, touching every thing, gently sensing the world around you. With each breath draw inspiration to your heart and feel connected to everything around you.

"With our eyes still shut, let's get our pencils and notebook ready. Okay, let's open our eyes! Describing whatever you see, hear, feel, touch or smell is fine to add to the poem."

Guide the group through the rest of the poem by prompting them to complete each line of the poem;

"To the East I ...
To the South I ...
To the West I ...
To the North I ...
Above I ...
Below I ...
Inside I feel ...
Altogether I am ...
I give thanks for all there is."

If it is appropriate, let the group to spend time decorating their poems with some natural colours from grass, earth, flowers, berries etc. Simply rubbing the colours on to the page can be quite effective. Allow them to mingle with friends and show off their work to each other.

When the poem is done, we gather everyone in and people are invited to share their poem with the group.

Chapter 4

Beyond the Big Five

As a child living in Kenya, 'the big five' meant lion, leopard, elephant, buffalo and rhino. On Sunday mornings, my sister and I would blearily get into our small car and mum would drive us into the game park just outside Nairobi for some early morning game spotting, hoping to see the big five.

Being in a wild place can really heighten one's awareness. Very rarely would we actually see all of the big five on one outing, and sometimes we saw very few of the bigger game animals at all; however we often experienced and happened upon many other delights in that wild place. Sometimes we would experience most by simply parking the car by a waterhole, winding down the windows fully, and waiting, watching, listening, as the natural rhythm of the day settled again after the disturbance of our arrival.

Later on in life I found that the best way to experience wildlife in England, with all the busy-ness of us humans going on, is to sit still in a pocket of wildness, clear my mind of its whirling thoughts, and settle into a state of natural awareness. Whilst in this kind of peaceful, relaxed state of being I have seen wonderful things like otters feeding, glow-in-the-dark fungi, a rowdy group of young wrens feeding inches from my nose and once, a terrified mouse hopped onto my foot as it was being chased by a salivating weasel! (Well, it was probably salivating, but it was moving far too fast for me to see clearly).

This chapter contains activities and games for expanding natural awareness using all five of our basic senses. By natural awareness I mean an awareness that is more childlike and in the moment. Relaxed yet alert, multi-faceted, and able to switch from all round to focused and back again in an instant. By doing these five activities many wonderful things will come into your body of experience too, by chance, as it were. There are also a few activities for developing other senses too, like intuition, balance and direction.

What are our senses?

One of the legacies of Aristotle is that here in the west we say we have five senses: of taste, smell, hearing, touch and sight.

Sense, broadly defined, is a faculty by which stimuli are perceived. There are many kinds of stimuli that we humans perceive, physical and non-physical, like temperature, pain, balance, movement, mood and magnetism, for example. There are also many stimuli that other animals can perceive that we can't. For example, bees can perceive polarised light, sharks sense electricity and cats and dogs know when you are coming home before you get there...which brings us to the senses of intuition and 'paranormal'. As you can see, without going into it deeply, there is much more to sense than smells, tastes, sounds, touches and sights.

Willow buds and tree reflections

Clouds of the mind, sensing with the heart

The human mind is a very busy and powerful thing. So much going on. So many thoughts. I sometimes find it very hard to get beyond the distractions of my mind and enter a place of natural awareness because I am constantly distracted by thoughts.

For a moment, imagine you are on a cliff top overlooking a wooded valley. There is a half moon, and a bright scattering of stars above. As you settle down to enjoy the night on a comfy sit mat, wrapping a blanket around you, a low mist starts to obscure the scene. First, the horizon is hidden. Then the moon and stars drift in and out of the picture and it becomes hard to settle your gaze on any one thing. Your eyes dart around looking for things to focus on, and the whole splendour of the night is marred by your irritation directed at the mist. The mist is like the mind. It can cloud the senses and stops us from being fully present in time and place. If we were to accept the mist for what it is, relax and expand our perception so that our depth of field of vision becomes more infinite we would see a whole shifting pattern of light and shadow across a beautiful landscape.

It can be very useful to have a simple technique or quick routine that stills the mind, and allows us to be more fully present when exercising our senses. One such technique is the Sacred Silence. It comes from the teachings of Stalking Wolf and Tom Brown Jnr., and is laid out in Tom's book *Awakening Spirits*. When done regularly it is short, sweet and effective. The basic idea of the Sacred Silence is to spend some time moving your awareness around each part of your body in turn, from your feet upwards, physically and mentally relaxing it, before physically and mentally relaxing your body and mind as a whole unit, and then finishing with a few deep breaths and centering your awareness on the beating of your heart. By then, you should be present, relaxed and ready for tracking!

Tracking, signs and asking questions

Out tracking for the day with Tom Schorr-kon on the Otter Valley

Tracking animals is what people did before humankind carved tablets and then started making books to read! Learning to read signs and to ask questions about what is going on outside us is hard-wired into our hereditary genetic material. It is necessary for survival. We are inquisitive.

Was that *really* Mrs Fox and Mr Badger out together last night?

At one time in the human race, we would have spent hours close to the earth, following a trail, hunting or foraging for dinner. We would have had to know where the animals were, which bushes were producing ripe berries, which leaves told of secret starch stored beneath the soil. Now we simply rush to the supermarket without even touching the earth beneath the tarmac. Since the industrial revolution 200 years or so ago, humans have become more and more town and city based. We have become increasingly solipsistic (go on! Track the word in a book of words!). So much of our questioning is focused on the human created environment as we are becoming increasingly divorced from the earth.

We move around in metal boxes, walk about on hard surfaces that leave little trace of our passing. Most of us watch news and read papers, no longer looking to the skies for a weather forecast, or into the fields to see which crops are ready to harvest. There is no perceived need to study the other, natural morning news; the tracks left during the night in the dust along the kerbside, the new pile of windblown leaves in the porch or patterns of clouds foretelling the weather. We are increasingly fed information, and told what events mean, leaving the inquisitive mind unexercised (in a wallpapered box).

However, unlike reading a book or watching telly, tracking involves the whole body and all the senses, and can be endlessly fascinating and completely absorbing. So much to see, so many questions to ask! Young people are naturally very inquisitive and have inner detectives, champing at the bit, waiting for an adult to mentor them through the process of finding out. With a questioning mind and sharp eyes, children make fantastic trackers. Every hole must be looked into.

Hello? Anybody in there?

What's this? What's *that*? Why? Everything in the world has meaning. Every nibble of a grass stem has marks from the set of teeth that made it. Every body has its own unique way of walking, talking and dressing. Every place has a feeling or spirit. Everything is a track or a sign to the tracker.

Who, what, why, where, when, how?

(I found it very interesting to note, that as I wrote this section of the book, my daughter went through a phase of butting into conversations and blurting out, as if all in one word: "whowhatwhywherewhenhow?" It's just something that was going on in the playground I'd guess...)

These six questions lead us to answers. We might still not find out *the* answer we want, but the questions *will* guide us through the process of seeking the answers, eliminating or revealing possibilities as we go.

Imagine for a second we are holding a hazelnut shell, about a foot in front of your nose. The nut has a hole in it. A couple of questions pop into our mind: who ate this and when? We ask a few questions of the nut and the hole. What made the hole in the shell? The nut has been gnawed, not pecked or broken open. **What does this mean** (probably the most important question of the lot)**?** From the information so far, we can say the creature that ate this nut was probably not a bird, or a human.

Looking at the teeth marks we can see that it was an animal that has sharp front teeth, because of the grooves radiating out from the hole, so probably a rodent such as a mouse or vole, but not one strong enough to gnaw and break the nut, like a squirrel or a rat.

Let's ask some more questions.

What kind of hole is it? Is it round or oval? Is it more of an oval than a round shape? Dormice usually make holes that are more round than oval. Where is the hole on the hazelnut? If it is nearer the base than the tip, so again, this is information that points to the nut being eaten by something other that a dormouse. The teeth marks are mostly in the direction of the tip of the hazel nut. There is no sign that the teeth have broken the shell. Voles have bigger teeth and stronger jaws than wood mice. So how can we tell whether it was a mouse or a vole? For this information, we can look outwards, at the bigger picture.

Where was the nut found? We found it on the ground, in a secluded spot, at the base of a fallen tree, under an overhang created by the exposed roots. We are standing in a fairly open wood, a fair distance from any thickets or bramble patches, the preferred habitat of a bank vole. So, the 'who?' that ate the nut was probably a wood mouse, but who exactly? Was it mister or missus mouse? And are they still alive? Oh! Is that their house over there with all those tiny nibbled nuts and seeds? We have asked so many questions and found out so many answers but we still don't know who ate the kernel of the nut and when they ate it!

Do you really want to find out? Well. For that we might just need to come back at dusk, on a moonlit night, and sit really still to find out, as well as undertaking an intense study of nut hole ageing!

To track or not to track? Questioning that goes deeper

The process of tracking and questioning can also be applied to our inner anatomy, physiology and psychology. As educators and mentors we are often presented with participants who have various physical and emotional symptoms, and we have to 'track' to find the cause of and solutions to these issues. There are many books on this, the more inner tracking field. My favourite, *Environmental Art Therapy and the Tree of Life* is by Ian Siddons-Heginworth. There are also many good books on tracking, tracks and sign on the market, for tracing in the physical world. See the section on suggested reading at the back of this book for a few more books if you are interested.

Tracking is such a huge and diverse subject that is *way* beyond the scope of this book, however I felt I must include *something,* so have included the following activity, for a bit of fun and to whet your appetite for tracking and start you logging up some dirt time.

Follow that log!
Ages 5 and up
Group size: up to 16
At least 20 minutes

Ready
Follow a log involves one of the students going off into the woods, dragging a log or a branch behind them to make an easy to follow trail, and then hiding somewhere. As they go, the plants are flattened and marks are left on the trails they take. The rest of the students, now known as the 'trackers', wait with their eyes shut and hands over ears until the hiding one stops moving. The trackers then have to go and find the hidden one.

Get set
A heavy, but manageable branch with twigs snapped off, leaving sharp bits to cut into the earth is one of the best things to drag. So are logs from a coniferous tree, like larch, with the resinous side branches still sticking out an inch or two. You may need a short length of rope too. The game works well either in small groups of 4-6 or larger groups of up to 16.

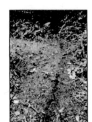

Look, she went that way! Round the corner, into the trees and...oh! .....
She has put the log is on the fire!

Go!
"This game is a bit like hide and seek. One person is going to run off into the undergrowth, dragging this branch, and then hide somewhere. Meanwhile we will all wait here, eyes closed, ears covered. When the person hiding is hidden, we will all come and find them. Ready?"

Choose someone who is sensible, agile and not too daring to go first, so they don't go too far away!

"Charlie, when I say go, I want you to go off and hide, somewhere just beyond the edge of our sight. Everyone else I want you to sit down, close your eyes and cover your ears, now. Ok, Charlie, Go!"

When Charlie is hidden, give the all clear.

"Alright everyone, open your ears and eyes. Let's work as a team to track him down. Which way do you think he went, and *why*?"

When 80% or more of the people in the team are agreed in the direction to go, we set off.

"Right. As soon as you are not sure which way to go on, stop, and we can look at the signs and decide as a team. Let's go!"

Useful things to know

As the trackers get used to the game, the level of difficulty can be increased by extending the distance the hiders go off into the woods, changing terrain (from, say, bracken, through leaf litter, to short grass moorland then areas with exposed rocks), and by using a lighter branch or log, which leaves a less visible trail to follow.

This game can be played in a very light hearted way with trackers instantly bounding off as soon as they are given the go ahead. Or, with just as much fun, a more teamwork based, problem-solving approach can be used, (which I outlined in the Go! Section).

You can also develop the game further by turning it into a silent movement activity (using the fox-walking skills you will learn in a later chapter). In this way of playing, the trackers try to get as close to the hidden one as possible, without alerting him to their presence. It is usually necessary for the tracking team to come up with a set of body and hand signals to facilitate their silent movement.

Another extension of the game is to give the person who goes off to hide a backpack containing a blindfold and water pistol. When they are hidden they put on the blindfold and listen for the approaching trackers.

Practising the art and science of tracking can involve a lifetime of study for one to become a master, and the more 'dirt time' a person has, asking '**what does this mean?**' the more likely they are to become an expert tracker, and have a great understanding of how nature, both inner and outer, works.

Tracking involves all our senses. To develop whole body awareness it is sometimes necessary to isolate our senses, exercise them individually, before re-assembling them in a more fully functioning whole, so lets move on to activities for the basic senses.

Activities for the Big Five

Sight: Soaring Eagles
Ages 4 and over
Groups size: up to 30
Time 15-60 mins

Ready
A day with a light wind is one of the best for developing peripheral, or wide-angle vision in the woods. The kind of day when leaves are trembling a little, branches and taller plants in the herb layer are waving slightly in puffs of breeze.

Wide-angle vision is also 'great depth of field' vision – Landscape photos are often taken with wide angle lenses and have a great depth of field to keep everything in focus. Such pictures have to be taken by a very still camera, with a long shutter exposure time and a tiny aperture. In the same way, we can develop wide-angle vision skills by encouraging our students to pretend they are a kind of animal which uses wide-angle vision. Being a deer or a rabbit would also be fine, but I rather like the idea of doing a bit of soaring to expand awareness so I always choose to be an eagle!

Get set

Assemble with your group in an area where they can all stand with their arms out to their sides.

Go!

"Okay everybody, let's raise our arms to shoulder height, out to the sides like wings. Wriggle your fingers. See if you can see both sets of fingers wriggling as you gaze softly ahead. Find the periphery of your vision by moving your wriggling fingers around the edges of your sight."

"Eagles soar high in the air to get a wide-angle vision of the landscape, where they can notice the movement of their prey over a wide area. Sometimes they will make use of rising columns of air, thermals, to soar effortlessly. Eagles, owls and other hunting birds will also perch on a high branch for hours, waiting for prey to move into their sight.

"Let's imagine we are a flock of eagles, move around each other, still gazing softly, soaring about in a thermal with only our wing-tip feathers ruffled by the breeze".

As we get into the feeling of this expanded, peripheral vision, I allow it to grow for a minute or two before saying.

"Lets come in to perch somewhere with a good view, to carry on hunting from." When everyone has landed;

"Look out across the landscape for movements using your special wide angle vision. Become aware of all the trembling, waving foliage, both near and far, and see the ripples of wind brushing across leaves and branches moving like waves on the seashore. Scan the landscape for prey. Look and listen for movement."

Spend as long as possible watching for 'prey'. Perhaps you will see small birds emerge from cover as a gentle stillness settles.

When the time is right, we fly back, up into the air and soar on to a place where we can all land and regroup to share the experience. I ask the group to offer words that describe what we felt as they soared, and what we saw as they perched, hunting for prey with our wide-angle vision.

Smell: The Snorting Sorting Game
Ages 6 and up
Group size: up to 35
About 10 mins for a group of 20

Ready, get set and Go!
This game uses the sense of smell to sort a large group of people into small groups. Say you need to separate 16 people into four groups. You will need a tissue for each person, and four distinctly different smelling essential oils, (e.g. Lavender, orange blossom, tea tree and vetiver) and enough pegs to peg out all the tissues on a line or fence. Apply a drop of each of the four smells to fours sets of tissues. Hang them out randomly. Ask your group to come along and take a tissue each, smell the tissue, and then find the other three people who have tissues that smells the same!

Touch: Blindfold Trail Following
Ages 7 and up (I am yet to try it with anyone younger)
Group size: 2-8 per leader
30 mins or more

Ready

One way to develop the sense of touch is to follow a trail or path through the undergrowth blindfolded. We humans spend so much time looking upon the world without ever touching or smelling it. So try this activity, it's fun. It's great for developing the sense of touch as you feel your way along the ground, sensing the hoof impressions in the soil with your fingertips, smelling the richness of the soil and the texture of rotting leaves or logs. Try feeling for nibbled grass stems and perhaps bramble tips. Notice the banks or walls to the tunnel of vegetation beside you, feel places where the moss has been worn off logs as feet and bellies have passed by.

Get set

Find a deer or badger trail through an area where dogs rarely go (for obvious reasons). Scout along it for anything you don't want to put your hands or knees in. Choose a trail that has defined edges, with dense undergrowth to the sides to minimise folks going off the trail. The length and sinuosity of the trail depends on the age and ability of the people you are with.

Go!

Find a trail. Simply get down on hands and knees and put the blindfold on. Off we go down the trail! There is no rush. Take time to really explore the world you are moving through, delight in the textures you find with your fingers.

Useful things to know

When working with groups it is best to leave a little time between each person as they set off. If you are doing this with little ones it can be a good idea to have someone looking on at various stages along the trail, and it's just as much fun to be watching! With little ones you can start off with a trail that is more like a tunnel in the undergrowth as little as two paces long. I have sometimes called the activity "the badger tunnel" and told children we are going to pretend to be badgers feeling our way through the tunnel. This activity can also be done with small groups of older, more independent individuals by allowing them to go off together, to find and follow a trail of their choice. Remind people to check for and remove ant ticks – if spotted quickly they often simply brush off.

Hearing: Deer Ears and Guard a Tree

Deer Ears
Any age
Any group size
A few moments

Ready, get set

To help us become more sensitive to sounds and the direction they are coming from we can put our cupped hands behind our ears to capture more sound. Get your group into listening for sounds more intently simply by saying "Deer ears!"

As a signal to do this I will often introduce the concept early on during an outing or camp, using a loud noise or an interesting sound to spark off the activity.

Go!

Upon hearing something, for example a green woodpecker calling, I turn to face the sound and cup my hands behind my ears and say,

"Listen! One way to listen for particular sounds is to give yourself 'deer ears'. These are deer ears! Stand facing me, and put cupped hands behind your ears, with the cups facing forward."
Slowly reducing the volume of my voice to a whisper,

"Most animals have ears that are mush larger than our and many animals can swivel their ears to locate sounds very precisely.

"Move your deer ears so they are facing the other way (like the chappie with his eyes shut on the extreme right of the photo). I show them by doing it myself, and continue to speak at the same quiet volume. Pointing my deer ears forward again I find out if anyone noticed the effects of swivelling their 'deer ears' and ask if anyone has ideas when deer ears might be useful.

Guard a Tree
Ages 6 and up
Group size: up to 30
At least 15

Ready

For this game, each tree has a blindfolded guardian spirit, who is armed with a water pistol to protect the tree from being touched by 'dastardly double demons'. If a double demon touches the tree with two hands, without being squirted by the water pistol, the tree will die.

Get set

You will need a water pistol that squirts water a long way, water to top it up with, a blindfold and a tree! Depending on the age and ability of your group, the tree should be surrounded by noisy, or quiet material underfoot, and have a varying degree of difficulty of obstacles on the way to the tree.

Go!

Our tree guardian has been chosen and is waiting, blindfolded, armed and alert by the tree.

"Now, form into pairs, putting your arms around each others waists to become Double Demons, and spread out around the tree, out of range of the water pistol, ready to begin!"

On the word, the demons move forward to try and touch the tree without getting squirted, while the tree guardian uses his powers of hearing to locate, squirt and destroy the demons. "GO!"

The game usually has a rapid turn around and even the most blindfold-shy folks want to have a go before the end. When played in conjunction with some of the sneaking skills you will learn later on with this book, the game tends to become less excited and giggly, and increasingly slow and stealthy.

Taste: Herb walk and Blindfold Snack Time!

Taking your group for a walk in the woods you are bound to encounter several different edible plants. Edible doesn't always mean 'tastes good'. Our ancestors will have been used to a more extreme range of tastes than us. If you know a plant is edible, it's best to approach wild food tasting with an open mind, and experience the taste for what it is, not whether it's 'nice' or not.

Going for a browse, with someone who knows, can be one of the most intimate ways to enter not only the realm of taste, but also the 'green wall' of the botanical world.

There are no 'ready, get set, go!' sections for these two activities. To lead a herb walk you really need to be sure of what you are encouraging folk to taste. In Britain, there are not actually many plants that will kill you by tasting, but enough to emphasise that you will need to be *really* sure!

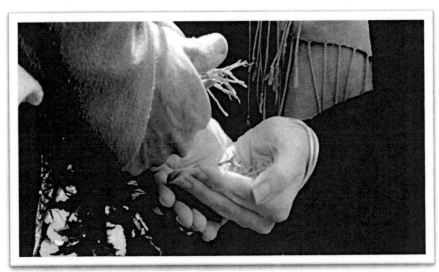
Mmm, marsh thistle roots – washed of course.

When trying out a plant new to me, unless I am 100% sure it is edible, I rub a bit on my lip first and then wait a moment or two. If there is no burning sensation, I will try a little on my tongue. Again, if this feels Okay, I will chew a bit, savouring and smelling without swallowing, spit the plant out, and wait a few minutes more before chewing a bit more and swallowing. In my backpack I usually carry two books for when I am on the trail, not sure of a plant, and want to look it up; a wild food guide and a botanical key to flowering plants.

For more details, either look in the reference section for plant identification guide recommendations, or book up on a course with an expert.

Hedge garlic or Jack in the Green in May.

Edible Plant list

What follows is a list (by no means comprehensive) of the common names of some easily identified edible plants. In the words of Pooh bear, consider it a little something to keep you going. If you are new to foraging it may be useful to chose a few plants to get to know at a time, rather than trying to learn the whole lot at once.

Wild Strawberry, Wild raspberry, Wild Gooseberry, Blackberry, Red and Blackcurrants, Bilberry– leaves, flowers and fruit, though the leaves are usually astringent.

Beech, oak, hawthorne leaves and pine needles are edible when limp and young, lime leaves all through the year.

Primrose, wood avens, wood sorrel, wood sage, nettle, white dead nettle, wild garlic, ground ivy, dandelion, hedge mustard, garlic mustard, great willow herb, sweet violet, the vetches, opposite leaved golden saxifrage, selfheal, mallow, cleavers, woodruff and stitchwort all have edible leaves and flowers.

Edible flowers include: wild rose, mullein and evening primrose.

Roots: Evening primrose, burdock, pignut, silverweed, dandelion and sweet vetch.

As you know, waiting for food makes it taste better, but somehow, so does being outside. The simple activity of having a blindfolded snack-time outdoors is great fun for the participants, less worrisome and troublesome when it comes to mess, and helps people really experience their food for its flavours and textures. I usually lead the session by simply asking, "Hey! Does anyone want to have a go at eating their snack blindfolded?" It usually works well.

So, moving onto some other senses...

Intuition and the Moccasin Game
Any age
Group size: up to 20
As long as you like, but at least 15 mins

Nights around the fire are a perfect time for this game.

Ready
Intuition has been defined as "the ability to sense or know immediately without reasoning." This kind of perception is invaluable to our lives and influences us more than most of us give credit for.

The moccasin game comes from the Native American Indian peoples. Many tribes such as the *Ojibwa and Shawnee* have played variations of this game. The version we play goes like this...

Get set
You will need a number of small easily identifiable objects, say eight. Each needs to small enough to be concealed easily within a shoe. Make sure they are all noticeably different from each other, for example a pinecone, a snail shell, an elastic band, a silver coin, a pen, some keys, a watch and a stick.

You will also need a blanket to display them on and a thick cloth or jumper to cover them with, and three or four shoes. If you want to keep score, you need a load of small sticks or stones to give out to those who get the answers right.

Choose one of the players to be a moccasin man.

Go!

"Everyone come and have a look at the objects on the blanket. Study them well!"

Allow a few minutes for this, then, cover up the objects.

"Everyone close your eyes apart from the moccasin man!"

The moccasin man chooses an object from under the cloth and places it in one of the shoes, so no one can see it.

"Game on!" (or something like that) "Players, use your intuition to sense, without reasoning, which object is hidden in which shoe. When one of you has an idea or feeling, stick up your hand and the moccasin man can ask for your answer. When the right object and the correct shoe is chosen, the round will be over".

This game is fun and can often go on for hours, rotating the moccasin man in a rhythm that suits your group - a great game for long nights and rainy days.

Balance and the Balance Beam
All ages
The more beams, the more people!
10 mins to an hour or so...

Everyone on at once! Thanks to Chris Salisbury of WildWise for the image.

Ready

We all know it's easier to stand on one foot with our eyes open than closed. This is because balance, or equilibrioception, involves other senses, such as our ability to see, perceive acceleration and to know where parts of our bodies are in relation to one another (proprioception, another long word!).

Having a good sense of balance is as essential to us everyday humans as it is to balance gods like surfers and unicyclists: basically, balance stops us falling over. When our sense of balance is interrupted, which can be for many reasons, we may feel dizzy, disoriented or sick. With a good sense of balance, we can travel more easily along the tightrope of life.

Get set

For this activity you will need a beam at least 4 metres long. Working in woods it is usually easy to find a fallen tree close to, or on, the ground.

All we did here was to level off the trunk, clear off the ivy. Hey presto! a balance beam (having prepared the beam the teenagers that made it did not want to leave it!). The nearer the beam is to the ground, the safer it is, obviously, and if you want to be more testing, simply build the beam off the ground by tying it to two vertical, living, tree trunks and support it in the middle. I am often surprised at how much rope I need to tie two trunks together with a square lashing, so have lots of rope! You may also want to have blindfolds at the ready.

Go!

There are many activities you can do on a beam. Here are a few:

- Walk forwards and backwards from one end to the other without falling off.
- Try with your arms behind your back.
- Now try it with a blindfold on!
- Try other ways of moving like hopping, crawling, sliding sideways, doing a jump, stopping half way and turning around. Of course, the gymnasts can try back flips, but they are not for most of us mere mortals.
- Combat: two opponents try to push or knock each other off. Again, many options - hands free, blindfolded, hands behind back, with armour and sticks...!
- Co-operative: try and get past someone else on the beam without falling off, move along as a caterpillar of people, try and get one team past another...

There are so many possibilities. Have fun, and be safe! And take a flask of tea in case you are there for a long time!

Direction: The Blindfold Drum Stalk
Age 7 upwards
Groups size: up to 20
At least 15 mins, and about 10 mins per round

Ready
A sense of direction, external and internal, physical and spiritual, can be developed through listening, questioning and feeling. Like all sense muscles, it needs exercising. If we limber up our sense of direction in our outdoor gym, using the physical sense of hearing, we can also move towards the more subtle directional sense of which path in life to follow (There's a little more about this in the next chapter).

The blindfold drum stalk is another activity that comes to me from the Stalking Wolf lineage of teachers. So I assume it is of Native American origin, but I am sure that the game is not exclusive to that part of the world. I have given it other names, like blundering zombies (because of all the blundering people with outstretched arms closing in on the drum beater), and more positively, blindfolded sneaking ninjas!

The basic idea is to make a sound the blindfolded participants travel towards. Changing the rapidity of the drumbeat, the distance travelled, and the terrain alters the level of difficulty – the less frequent the beats, the further the sound has to travel and the more obstacles, the harder it gets.

As the players get more adept, they should hopefully resemble silent stalking ninjas rather than zombies...

Get Set

You will need something that makes a noise that will carry a reasonable distance. I often use a drum with a good bass sound, or two sticks that click well together, but a bell or saucepan lid would do. You will also need blindfolds, something that doesn't cover the ears too! Some helpers – a ratio of about 1 helper to 5 or 8 participants is about right.

Choose a large flat circular area free of trip hazards to begin with, and work up to thickets, bogs, slopes and overgrown areas! It is amazing how the awareness of people develops as they relax into the activity and sense their way about the place, not just with their sense of touch.

Go!

To play we hand out a blindfold to each participant, then divide the group into helpers and participants. Each helper then organises their group into a caterpillar to follow behind them.

"Blindfolds on! One hand on the shoulder of the person in front of you! The helpers will lead you to the place you are going to start from!"

When everyone is in place around the perimeter, the beater, standing in the middle, bangs the drum, at a rhythm of about 1 beat every 10 seconds, and the participants have to make their way back towards him. This continues until the last of the players is back in. The helpers are on the lookout for people wandering into trees and help re-direct those that may be blundering or panicking.

When everyone is in, we quickly review what the participants found hard and easy by asking questions like: How did the ground feel? Were they unsteady? Did anyone sense a tree *before* they bumped into it? Did anyone find a way of moving that felt really good?

Once become familiar with the game, it can be extended by changing the 'pitch' size or by positioning all the participants in a line, along a woodland ride for example. The beater chooses a suitable place off in the woods for the participants to come towards. When the participants are more practised, make the terrain more difficult, try a boggy area for example, or try doing a blindfold shallow river-crossing drum stalk!

It is also interesting to drum stalk with a minimal amount of clothes on. I am not saying you should strip off completely! Shorts, bare feet and perhaps a tee shirt is good. Our awareness increases when we have more skin exposed, so we can move more sensitively and silently through the landscape.

Chapter 5

Where am I? Aidless Navigation and Ways of Lost-Proofing Ourselves

This chapter is about aidless navigation systems, ancient ways of finding your way about the landscape and sharing the information with others. Through the practice of bushcraft and skills that are close to Nature we are bound to come into contact with ways of not getting lost, like using the stars, following rivers downstream, using shadow sticks, journey sticks, 'songlines', sea swells, and the qualities of the winds to find direction.

We are also likely to come across people who believe there is more to life than the world we see around us. I am one of them, and I believe there is also the inner world and the journey of the spirit, whose path is mapped out on the realm of myth and story. So this chapter is also about ways to help you find your soul path, or sense of direction in life, as I believe that by knowing where we are in the outer world helps us get our bearings in the inner world. When an instinctual sense of direction is combined with heightened awareness of what is going on in the here and now, both on an outer and inner level, we have a greater chance of choosing the 'right' path for ourselves, and the landscape we live among.

My story: Getting lost to find myself.

Twelve years ago I went on a kind of walkabout and vision quest, revisiting some of the places of my childhood, hoping to get a sense of what to do in life. I found that in the Southern Hemisphere I lost my instinctive sense of where North is and often had to resort to a compass or map and really think about where the sun went down in order to face the opposite way to do my morning stretches. Anyway, I ended up on a mountain in Australia, close to the area where my dad had worked when I was two or three (he took me with him), with a hammock, blanket, mozzie net and a load of cucumbers (for water because I didn't feel I could go three days and nights without water). I made camp, made a magic circle to stay within, and prayed for a sense of direction in life.

When I came down from the mountain to a gorgeous, warming sunset (it had rained all the time I was up the mountain and I was soaked through) I had a sense that my path is as a teacher, not a class teacher or a P.E. teacher, not an environmental science teacher either, but some kind of teacher. The next part of my journey was to find out. A year later, I started teaching didgeridoo in a private Primary school in England and at the same time came upon the Primitive living and Survival skills courses taught by Tom Schorr-kon. A few years after that I became self-employed doing what I do now, learning to play, playing to learn! I am so thankful for the time I spent alone, in the places of my ancestors, admitting I was lost and asking the flow of life to show me a way forward.

Going off into the woods to look for edible and medicinal plants.

Ways of sharing where I am

Many animals know where their larders, their food sources, are, and will follow some kind of habitual pathway to get to them. Some animals share the information, with dance or smell for example. For humans, being able to create a map that others can understand is a very useful skill. When I look at an OS map, I imagine I can soar up like a buzzard, high above the landscape, and visualise the lie of the land. I can also swoop down to see cliffs or churches up close. Being able to remember a journey and give understandable directions is another vital skill ("ahrrr, then, from the old oak with the lightning strike go over to the rock-face that looks like a head and there, at the base, you shall find the sweetest pool, edged with watercress, brimming with trout!").

A post graduate researcher friend was telling me that ants teach each other how to find food sources by remembering a route and then leading other ants in the colony, one by one, to the food source, until a tide of ants is all working for the greater good of the colony. Bees dance to tell other bees where to find the nectar they collect, and all kinds of plants and creatures use scent as a way of letting other creatures know where they are.

Humans, like many other creatures have inbuilt ways of knowing 'where I am' and sharing information on the location of resources, often in an artistic way through song, dance, mark-making and sculpture, (like the spokes of a wheel activity earlier in the book and the aerial map making activity later on in the chapter). But does this really help with our spirit's journey to happiness? Knowing where you are in life is more than plotting your place on a two dimensional map, it also has to do with listening to your sense of direction, that little voice inside that knows the way.

It's well known that not everyone thinks they have a sense of direction - a sense of orientation in space or a voice inside they can hear. For some people it is loud and clear and some people have a sense of direction only in areas they know well, while many people are lost most of the time! Some people get lost in the wilderness, while others get lost in life. So, what actually is a sense of direction and where is it found, because there are no actual organs or receptors associated with it, and it is more than simply a physical thing.

Some may say it is a general awareness of what is where. Some will say it is tuning in to the magnetic field of the earth or being able to read your dreams. Others will say it is also knowing where the sun is, what the time of day is, the time of year...while yet others will say it is instinct, some kind of internal homing device.

Praying for direction.

Many Muslims will be able to tell you where Mecca is at any time of day, because they need to face Mecca to pray, five times a day. For some people, like myself, it is important to face the morning sun to do my early morning yoga. Each of the directions has a certain medicine, power or spirit that each of us can feel individually and personally The Native American Medicine Wheel is a wholistic way of seeing the cycle of life and life's lessons that is based on the directions of East,

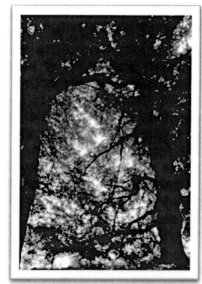

The Wildwood is rooted in myth as *the* place people get lost in...leaving a trail of breadcrumbs won't get you home again!

West, South, North, above, below and within. Different religions offer different, yet often very similar, paths to contentment. Even non-religious people say that it is important to make life choices that keep your spirit happy, your body and mind well, to live your dreams. There are also messages from the spirit world and the dream world to help us plot the course. Each place has its own 'dreaming'. Finding a sense of direction in a moment can be as simple as finding the place one feels most comfortable to sit down in, and getting into the 'spirit of the place'. I sometimes forget I don't have to be going anywhere to be in the 'right place at the right time! Stopping still and listening is just as important as the moving about. In some cultures, learning to listen to the direction of the spirit, and the land, is so vitally important to the health of the community that individuals are encouraged to pray, do a Vision Quest or go walkabout and literally ask the land or spirit of life for a sense or vision of what to do (with their life) for the greater good of all.

"When you take a man from his land, you take his life spirit"
Aborigine, Australia.

Continual awareness of what is where and what things mean, helps build up a picture of what lies in which direction. By spending time on the land, being more part of it, and tuning into the power, or medicine of Nature, we are more likely to be acting in accordance with the way of the world, the Dao as some folks call it, and be able to follow a path in life that suits us *and* the land best.

Much of the time we spend in cities, in front of the TV, being immersed in contemporary culture, we are bombarded with adverts telling us that happiness is this or that way, confusing the sense of direction, maybe with drugs and alcohol, and knocking the spirit off track. I think it isn't surprising at all that many people feel lost in their lives.

Helping us find our way

Not all human-generated information is confusing, some information is actually meant to help steer the soul on its path. For thousands of years people have shared news and told myths relating to the survival of humankind, the trials, tribulations and joys of life. Within the stories are clues, many levels of meaning, to help us choose the path. We have many celebrations, ceremonies and festivals to mark the passage of time and the specialness of events, which serve as marker posts for and reminders of the cyclical nature for our life's journey. Somewhere, inside each one of us, is a voice that knows the way forward.

Developing a sense of direction

When out and about with a group I will often stop and ask questions like, "Can you hear that goldcrest?" "Where is Camp?" or "Where is North?" On a cloudy day I will ask, "Where is the sun?" I could just as easily ask: "Where is the nearest source of water?" It's useful to know where basic survival needs are at any one time as it brings a settled sense of safeness, and peace to the spirit. It's a bit like having a full log shed, or a pantry full of food, if you know what I mean. I believe that being aware of what phase the moon is in, where the wind is coming from and being aware of what we feel like when walking into a new place or situation is using our sense of direction receptors. Wherever we are and whatever we are doing, there is information about things going on in the cycle of our lives, pointing to a way forward. We simply have to track it. So which way would you choose at a crossroads? The following activity may give you an idea of the answer, if you didn't know it already.

Which way do you walk?
Any age over 7
Group size: Up to 30
About 30 mins

Ready

It is said that a person lost in a relatively flat uniform habitat, where he can't see a point the distance to head towards, is likely to circle back on himself within a square mile. Why? Because we are usually left or right dominant. What does that mean? Well, it means that when we set off we will usually lead with one leg most of the time and spend a fraction longer on our favourite leg, which alters our stride length. When we leap we will favour one leg to land on first, when we come to a fork in a trail we will tend to choose one direction over another. To test 'dominance' in your students can be a fun activity in itself. It involves blindfolded participants walking a short way towards an object and seeing which way the participants veer off.

Get set

You will need a flat area about 30 paces long and 20 paces wide, clear of obstacles with something to aim for at the far end, like a tree or post. Check that there are no holes for people to twist ankles in.

You will need blindfolds for at least five people and a stick to mark the starting place.

Go!

We gather about 30yds away from the chosen tree or post, and place the stick upon the ground to mark the start.

"Do you know most of us do not walk in a straight line with our eyes closed? Most of us a naturally right or left dominant. If we are right handed our right arms tend to be bigger than our left. The same goes for our legs. We tend to push off and kick a ball with our favoured foot. So it is that when we have to make a choice, we tend to choose one way over the other. It is said that a person who is lost in a forest will circle back on his or herself in a square mile. This activity is about finding out which way we walk!"

"Who wants to go first?"

Squaring up their shoulders so they are pointing directly towards the tree and have the first volunteer walk off, carefully, in the direction of the tree. Keep an eye on them, and shout "Stop!" when they get close to where the marker tree is.

"Leave your blindfold on until the other participants have had a go."

Let the next four people have a go, making sure to stop participants who are going to bump into each other of course! When ready, give the command "Blindfolds off!" It is very interesting and often quite funny to see who veers off in which direction and by how much.

When we know which direction an individual is likely to favour it is useful to make a mental note in case they wander off.

This 'finding out our natural dominance' activity can be extended by putting weight on the back of the blindfolded person...giving another participant a piggy back is often a suitable and fun way to do this. Carrying a weight tends to exaggerate the veering off tendency.

Aerial Maps
All ages
Group size: up to 30
Up to 2 hours

Ready

One of the activities I enjoy most is making a sculpture map of the countryside around the place where I am working with my group, using found objects.

There are several ways of doing this, but it is always advisable to check an OS map first...so that you at least know in what direction the main landscape features are.

There are three main elements to a sculpture map:

- Something that represents the group
- The cardinal directions, E,S,W,N.
- Noticeable landscape features – like hills, churches, roads, big trees, ditches, etc

There is no fixed scale to a sculpture map. Depending on the skills and focus of the group you are working with, a map can vary from messy and vaguely useful to highly accurate and artistic. Our job as leader is to guide the process and inspire the group to have fun and create something they are proud of!

Get set

Choose an area where you can see at least some landscape features in the distance. With, or without a map in front of you, imagine you are a bird of prey, soaring high up above the land. Looking down you can see the countryside stretching out around you. You can see key features, like lakes, woods, villages, hedges, roads and estuaries. Spiralling back down, the land around you becomes fixed in your brain.

Go!

Representing the group.

To make an aerial map we start by getting everyone in a toe to toe circle. A straight stick is then stuck a short way into the ground in the middle of the circle.

"You have heard of the North and south Poles? This is our Centre Pole! We are going to make a map of the important features of this landscape, here and now. We are all standing around the pole. Let's all find a small stick to make a ring of sticks around the central pole."

Marking out the cardinal directions.

"The North and South poles are actual places, the East and West are more 'directions' than places. How do we find out where North is?"

Someone says, "Use a compass!"

"North is easy to locate with a compass, but remember that magnetic north is different to true north. In the Northern Hemisphere there are other ways of finding out which way North is, and the most reliable way during the day is to measure the length of shadow thrown by a stick placed vertically in the ground. The shortest shadow is thrown when the sun is highest in the sky, due south. However, you need the sun to be shining!"

"The other way to find true North is to look for the star that stands still, the North Star, and most survival books will tell you us to do that. What they won't tell us is one of the Paiute Nation legends from North America associated with the North Star."

"The story goes that an ancestral goat, who was a fantastic climber, in fact the best in the land, climbed to the top of a particularly high and dangerous pinnacle of rock one day. Having reached the top, he found that he could not get back down without jumping, which would mean certain death. Staying on top of the spire would also mean death, from starvation, because not enough grass grew there to keep the goat alive. He was stuck at the tip of the rocks, not knowing what to do, unable to move. When the goat brother cried out for help from the top of the spire, the Creator took pity him, carried his spirit high in the sky, turned it into a star, and placed it where all the other

127

stars move around it. So it is, to this day people navigate by this star, and some remember to give thanks to their goat brother, whose spirit unceasingly guides travellers."

"You may think that the best way to find out where East is involves getting up at dawn, but that doesn't necessarily reveal the position of East. The sun only rises due East at the equinoxes, around the 21st of March and September. So, the best way to locate East is by finding North first, then drawing a line to the centre of your circle and then going equidistant past the centre to mark the South. East and West can then be marked off by crossing this line at right angles."

(After that long lecture it is time to mark out the four main directions!)

"Who is standing in the North of our circle?"

"Cleo, I want you to find a suitable something to be the North Pole. It can be a stick or a rock..." Have Cleo place it on the outer edge of space you are making the map in.

A line is then drawn in the earth from the North Pole to the centre Pole and beyond to mark out the South Pole. The person in the place of the South Pole can go off and get a South Pole. We can then mark out the East and West.

To mark out East and West I ask the participants to think of a colour that represents the direction to them, and to then go and find little bits of that colour in nature to place at the edge of the map... often it is sunrise yellows for the East and Sunset reds for west.

Noticeable features.

When the cardinal directions are on the map on the ground then we can start adding noticeable features to the map. Exactly what type of noticeable features rather depends on where you are... it may be a village, school buildings, a road, a church, a river... you are probably limited only by your knowledge of your place and your model making skills. Good luck, have fun!

Songlines or Rap-Maps

Ages 7 and up
Lots of people!
An hour or more, especially with large groups

Ready

'Songlines' is a story, song or 'rap-map' making activity inspired by an aboriginal Australian perspective on the world. Australia's indigenous peoples believe that all life begins with the Dreaming or Altjeringa (in some Indigenous languages), which is also called the Dreamtime, a 'once upon a time' era long ago when archetypal ancestral totemic spirit-beings formed the World. These shape-shifting spirits embodied the forms of animals, plants, people, natural phenomena and/or inanimate objects. Proof that they existed comes from their formative journeying and the signs they deposited through the landscape. Their dreaming and journeying trails are the Songlines.

I have been told that the dreamtime still goes on today and that all plants and living creatures, including humans, continue to alter and change the world around us through our actions, and when we die, our bodies return to the earth, and our spirits return to the spirit of the land, which is why the earth is sacred. It is also why Aboriginal Australian people 'sing' the world into existence, when they travel on the land or go 'walkabout', by retelling the stories of the landscape as they travel on foot over it.

Making up songs, poems and raps about the journey to a hidden treasure is the skeleton of this activity, and it is fleshed out with observational and descriptive skills, working with others, some healthy competition and information recall and clothed with some opportunity for fun and laughter. It is another fine example of whole body learning about the land!

Get set

Collect a treasure for each group. I like the treasures to be something needed for another activity you plan to do that day –perhaps some spindles and bags of tinder for making fire by friction. However, as the activity can take a while, the treasures could be a variety of things for snack time, like tea bags, fruit and shortbreads. Whatever they are, keep them secret or at least disguised, so that only when all the treasures are found, brought together and revealed does the next activity become apparent.

Go!

Splitting the group into two or more teams, we make sure that each team includes an adult who knows how the activity works.

"Okay, everybody! Please choose a name for your team!"
Once the names have been decided give each team a treasure.

"Here is a treasure I would like you to place, some way off. It is meant to be found, so don't bury it, please! As you go on your way, looking for somewhere to place the treasure, I want you to make up a rap-map or a songline that leads to the treasure. So, for example, here is one I prepared earlier," (to be said in a Caribbean style to get 'de lilt of de verse').

> "Off to the east,
> taking 45 steps,
> and come to rest, at tall straight tree.
> Look to your left.
> What do you see?
> A holly bush, and a blackthorn tree.
> Walk between the two,
> down to the stream,
> cross it at the place where it's easy to jump,
> off a hump,
> climb up the bank,
> to the big ferns, three.
> Hop along the rocks,
> up the hill,
> 'til you find a warren but no rabbits to kill.
> Look in the holes,
> and you will find,
> the treasure you seek, of some kind!"

"When you have hidden the treasure come back and we will get together and teach each other the raps, stories or songs."

The groups have returned.

"Take turns teaching your rap map to one of the other teams. Find a technique for learning and remembering the new rap-map on you own. If you really are stuck I can give you some ideas".

I suggest standing in a row, with each person learning a line or two, or to try threading or tying something onto a string to remind them of the rap's lines.

When they are ready, send them off! When everyone has returned successfully the treasures can be unwrapped, or revealed to the rest of the group (because they have already been unwrapped!). Putting all the treasure items together everyone now knows what the next activity is and, what's more, the fun doesn't end there, because the rap-maps can be used later for a bit of fireside entertainment!

Find my magic map spot
A map-making activity for pairs
Up to 30
Ages 7 and up
30-45 mins

Ready
The purpose of this activity is to practise drawing a map in such a way that someone else can understand it. Working in pairs, each person goes and sits somewhere, draws a map of the surrounding landscape features and then swops their map with their partner. They then have to go and find the 'magic spot' in which their partner drew their map. Sounds simple...

Get set
Clip boards and paper and pencil for everyone (or card and felt tip pens...) Sit mats if it is damp under bum. Choose a defined area, preferably with a variety of features like big trees, bushes, grassy patches, rocks and ridges. About the size of a football pitch is about right for 30 people.

Go!

"Okay everyone, choose a partner."

"We are now going to play a game called 'find my magic map spot'. Each of you must go and find a place to sit down where you can't see your partner. This is your magic map spot. You then have ten minutes to draw the best treasure map you can, starting with an arrow to mark the spot you are sitting in, and the direction you are facing to draw the map (in relation to a distant object like the sun, a big tree or something on the horizon. Mark in all the noticeable landscape features you can, to help your partner find your magic spot. This game is about making it as easy as possible for your partner. What do I mean by noticeable landscape features?"

At this point tease out of the group the kinds of things that would be helpful to go on the map, starting with the larger landscape features.

"So, here's is a clipboard and a pencil for everybody. Draw things to scale, include paths, ditches, ridges, hedges – that kind of thing. Remember, before you leave, to mark the spot with a real arrow or 'x' made from two sticks or by scratching it in the earth, and then come on in. Don't tell your partner what the 'X was made from, so you can check with them to find out if it is the correct place! Good luck!"

When maps are swapped allow five minutes maximum for finding each other's places. This part can be done in a couple of ways… either by letting the pairs find each other's places one at a time, with one person guiding the other, doing the "warmer"/"colder" thing, or for older children and adults, by sending them off in different directions at once to find the x and find out what it is made from.

When everyone has finished we gather together to find out what makes a good map, and get ideas on how we can improve our maps next time.

"How many people want to play again?"

Here it is! My magic map spot!

Chapter 6

Sneaking

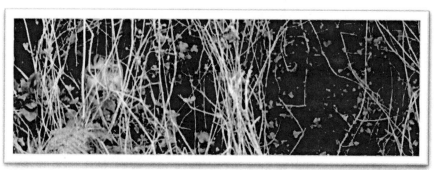

Who's that hiding in the bushes?

This chapter is about learning to walk quietly, to slip away into and through nature unnoticed.

My granddad was in the British secret (sneakret!) services during the Second World War. One of the things I remember most about him, apart from his wonderful 'shortcuts' (!), was that when we were out and about having a walk he would often sneak off without my knowing and then jump out shouting "BOO!" It was how he earned his name 'Bodad'.

Being able to slip off unnoticed and move silently, invisibly is a skill that can take years of fun to develop, to the benefit of both the sneaker, and the victims who learn to move about with more awareness. Such skills are essential to successful wildlife watching or hunting and involve the application of heightened awareness and a lot of body control.

Sneaking for wildlife watching is best done alone, and can be so very rewarding. Conversely, sneaking about trying to get a glimpse of wildlife with a big group is nigh impossible. You can probably imagine, moving along a path towards a known deer feeding ground, without talking, is hard enough for a small group of excited young children, let alone moving so slowly and silently that the feeding deer doesn't stop nibbling the dewy grass and become alert to their presence, and then bound away before the group arrives, leaving only a dungy offering!

Stomping, the Modern Way of Moving

"The earth is like the skin of a drum." Tom Schorr-kon

The shoes we wear influence the way our feet touch the earth. With each footfall a vibrational pattern spreads through our bodies and into the ground. Most of us are probably 'heel stompers' because of the kinds of shoes we have on our feet (By this I mean that the first point of contact with the ground is the heel). As our heel impacts with the ground a shockwave of energy, much reduced by the foam and rubbery materials in our shoes, is transferred into our bones and dissipated through the rest of our body. Every step is a judder. Many of us spend a lot of time walking from A to B on flat tarmac or stone surfaces where there is no need to place each foot carefully. Roadrunners tend to suffer more impact related injuries than cross-country runners because of the hardness of the surface.

Our bodies weren't originally designed to move they way they do now - with shoes stuck on the feet. However, I am sure we are evolving and adjusting to our new appendages! When our feet are trussed up in walking boots, with ankle support, laced half way up our calves, our feet can't always work to their full potential. Our footwear tends to bite into the earth to get a grip, and when we go from a man made to a natural surface without adjusting the way we walk there can be a lot of excessive erosion, especially as there are so many of us in this small country. So we turn the eroded area into a man made one...and slowly, as one folk singer put it, we are turning the earth from paradise into a parking lot.

It is said we learn how to walk by watching our elders. As a kid in Africa I played out in bare feet a lot of the time, as I am sure children of Britain did not so very long ago, so I feel very happy to be moving about that way. I was surprised to find out that is not always the case for everyone else. Many people here in the UK don't even touch grass or bare earth with their feet once a year!

What kind of example are we setting for our children, and is it important? Is it OK to wear shoes that mean we don't feel anything we tread on? Is it right that people go through life without walking on grass, stomping in clay or even having that icky

feeling of stepping on a slug and having it squidge between their toes? And is it right that our feet get so sensitive from wearing shoes that we can no longer bear to touch bare earth with the skin of our feet? No, surely that is just not right! I think we all need to learn how to walk softly, it's for the greater good of all for us all to make full use of our feet and, occasionally, create a slow and gentle beat on the earth drum.

Learning to Walk and Stalk

During my early twenties, I studied Tai Chi for a while. Later on, I studied with Tom Schorr-kon of Trackways who passes on teachings collected and handed down by a Lipon Apache elder, Stalking Wolf. During these times I learnt a new way of moving; slowly, surely, quietly and with awareness, the Fox Walk. Go on, have a go! Now! Dare you! (If you can do it without losing your balance while reading these instructions at the same time you will be on your way to becoming a master!)

Fox walking and stalking steps are best done in bare feet (or thin-soled shoes), using the bones, muscles and sensitivity of your feet to their full potential.

Lift up one leg until your thigh is parallel to the ground. Then let the foot come down softly to the ground so the ball, not the heel, touches first. The bones and tendons will stretch slowly to take your weight, minimising the shockwaves going through body and earth. Spread your weight along the outer edge of your foot to the heel, and when your body weight is all on this foot, slowly lift up the other foot, as a heron does, from the top of the ankle, to repeat the process again with the other leg. As you move, especially if there are other people, obstacles or trees and undergrowth around, you will be developing spatial awareness and exerting great body control. Your awareness spreads as you feel your way through your feet, becoming aware, with the edge of your vision, for suitable places for your feet to fall, and negotiating branches with, slow, whole body movement.

Concentric rings in Nature, an example:
Imagine you dropped a pebble into a pond. The ripples spread to the edges. A similar thing happens when an action disturbs the average goings on of a place. Say you step on a stick that snaps... a wren in a the brambles freaks and calls out it's alarm song. The pheasant a bit further away calls out too, because the wren has. The deer get up quietly and move deeper into the thicket and a passing crow looks down into the trees towards you, before swerving away, and the ripple passes on through the grapevine...

With Tom, we played sneaking games and moved more slowly than shadows. We practised making the least amount of disturbance to the concentric rings of nature, in an attempt to be invisible in the landscape. It meant going into a different reality, a different time zone. Nature Time. The Dreamtime. And in that time/place it becomes very noticeable that the way we walk affects nature in a big way. Now I can see a bigger picture and think that all this rushing around on tarmac needs to be balanced with a lot of agility, treading lightly and slowly on the earth.

The fox walk is a way of walking that produces a quiet beat on the drum skin of Nature. It's a way of moving that fits in well with the general rhythm of nature and so is a great way to see wildlife and listen to birdsong.

Once, as I was fox walking along a hedgerow at the edge of a scrubby field, a fox got up from where it had been dozing. It stretched and sloped off, in no particular rush at all, under a low holly branch. I had not really disturbed it, just got too close for comfort. If I had been wandering along at a usual walking pace, the fox would have been long gone before I reached its resting place. As we slow down to nature speed and allow our whole-selves to be present, we can re-focus on the world outside to develop peripheral awareness, and allow our brain waves to change. We create less of a bow wave as we move through time and space, and we are then more likely to enter the moment, The Dreamtime, Nature Time, to be part of the natural rhythm of things.

Sneak up on your own ideas

When fox-walking I certainly find a great deal of peacefulness, inner stillness and some kind of enigmatic re-juvination. Sometimes I get ideas, have insights and inspiration, because I am moving slowly enough, and quietly enough, to notice them; the wild ideas on the inside, as well as the wildlife on the outside. Fox walking is one of the ultimate walking meditations, being totally present and aware, moving very slowly and blending into the landscape. You too will see more wildlife and feel enlivened if you give it a go. As a bonus, you will certainly become more adept at sneaking up and surprising your mates or students.

So, how can we develop these essential sneaking skills in our children? Why, with the use of two essential forest school tools; the blindfold and the water pistol. And a few games of course!

Games such as the ones outlined below work for both the sneakers and the soakers. The sneakers develop their silent movement skills. The soakers develop their awareness and 'hunting' skills. This is true survival of the 'fittest' and 'wisest' in action!

The Sneaking Circle
Ages 5 and up
Group size: More than 5, less than 30 for most fun
At least 20 mins!

Ready
This game involves people sneaking into a circle to collect a treasure guarded by a blindfolded person armed with a water pistol. It is a very popular game, enjoyed by both children and adults. And it can go on and on and on...

Get set
You will need at least 5 players, a blindfold, a water pistol (a washing-up liquid bottle with the nozzle on will do but is hard for younger hands to squeeze), extra water for refills, and some treasure - something noisy to pick up like a bag of crisps, bell, bunch of keys...that kind of thing. Perhaps a towel for drying off wet faces and spectacles.

Go!
"Lets' get into a circle!" The ring needs to be big enough so that the people on the perimeter stand just outside the range of the water pistol.

We choose a 'guardian' to start in the middle, and stand guard over the 'treasure' that is on the ground, in the middle of the circle. They are given a blindfold and a large super soaker water pistol pumped up and ready for action. Stand clear (or not!) and ask them to have a quick test!

"Pop your blindfold on. Are you ready?"

"Is everyone else ready? Okay, sshhh! Let's be quiet!"

When there is relative silence, someone from the ring of participants is chosen to start sneaking in...

The players in the ring are chosen one at a time, to see if they can sneak in to the centre of the circle, pick up the noisy treasure and get back to the edge of the circle without being heard and being squirted. People who dash in and out are usually disqualified. If there are a lot of people in the ring, more than one person can be chosen to sneak in at the same time. You can decide how and how often you change over the guardian.

When play time is over, we have a brief closing circle to find out things like which sneaking techniques work best, who was the best listener, and of course, what can we learn from this?

Sneaky Assault Course

This game is an extension from the last one. The idea is for one person at a time to sneak along a narrow path, past a blindfolded person with a water pistol, without getting wet.

The assault course makes the trail more difficult; try putting things like crunchy leaves, twigs, branches on the path, add ropes, trip wires, webs of string with bells on... go on, be creative! It can be as much fun making the course, when your players are familiar with the game, as actually playing it. And of course, you don't have to have just one blindfolded person with a water pistol! You can have another blindfolded person with earplugs and a bucket of slop sitting right in the middle of the path for example!

To test agility even further, you could challenge the sneakers to carry a full cup (or even more difficult, a bowl) of water through the course and measure water levels at the end to find the most superior sneaker!

Bird Nests and Foxes (or hedgehogs or meerkats, or any other egg-eating predator)
Ages four and up
Up to 30
About an hour

Ready
The object of this game, based on hide-and-seek, is for the nest makers to make a nest on the ground to hide in, and for the foxes to find the nests and collect eggs. The ground nesting birds must sit completely still, waiting and watching. Their stillness keeps their eggs safer. It's necessary to have a couple of helpers to oversee the game and to help make nests, to assist with the camouflage and keep an eye on the action.

Get set
You will need to clearly mark out a nesting territory using string, ticker tape or a natural boundary of some sort, perhaps a little copse, or a clearing in the woods (to make sure no one goes off into the distance to hide, and is never seen again!). As a size guide, about half a football pitch of quality cover is about enough for a group of thirty 7-10 year olds. Make sure there are plenty of places to hide.

You will need a pot of mud, some charcoal and, a bag of hazelnuts or walnuts in their shells, and several helpers.

Go!
Dividing the group into two teams of foxes and birds, at a ratio of about 1 fox to every 4 or 5 birds, send the nest builders to go off and have 15-20 minutes to make a nest each and camouflage themselves before sitting still, on their eggs. For the eggs, I use nuts in their shells. Each bird is given four or five eggs, when they have made their nest. If there is a person who really doesn't want to play being a fox or a pheasant, they could be a stork, and deliver the eggs when the nest is made and the birds are settled in!

Meanwhile the Foxes can get camo'd up with some mud, charcoal and leaves stuck onto the mud and practise their sneaking skills... perhaps by playing grandma's footsteps on all fours!

When the nest-building time is up, the foxes to sneak in as quietly as possible and find nests from which to collect eggs. The more quietly the foxes sneak, the greater chance of catching a bird unawares.

Shhhh! Be still! The foxes are coming!

The foxes are only allowed to sniff the birds on their nests when they find them. If a bird flinches or moves anything other than its eyes while the fox is sniffing, then the bird has to give the fox an egg. The fox must then move on and the bird gets another chance to practise sitting very still. The foxes can only collect one egg from each nest. If a bird does not move at all, doesn't flinch, then it doesn't have to pass on an egg and well done to that bird for not flinching in the face of danger! After a time, the players can swop round and after a few rounds you can all get together and crack the eggs for a feast.

Capture the flag
Ages 10 upwards
Group size: 10 or more
At least 30 mins

Ready
Capture the flag is a traditional outdoor game with many variations played by older children and sometimes adults where two teams each have a flag (or other marker). The objective is to capture the other team's flag, located at the team's 'base', and bring it safely back to their own base. Enemy players can be 'tagged' by players in their opponent's home territory; these players are then, depending on the agreed rules, out of the game, members of the opposite team, or 'in jail'. One variation of the game includes a 'jail' area in addition to the flag on each team's territory, close to the middle line separating the two halves of the pitch.

Get set
You will need two soft frisbees, two flags (jumpers on sticks will do) and two 10m lengths of rope.

Go!

"Quick! Someone is coming from over there on the right!"

The game we play involves the flags being placed in a tag free zone marked off by a rope laid in a circle, so that the capturers have somewhere to be, without getting tagged, when they have reached their opponents' flag.

The flag has a soft frisbee at its base, and it is the frisbee that has to travel back to the base of the team who captures it, for a team to win the game. Players can run with, and throw the Frisbee. Each player has three lives. When a player is tagged they have to go to a jail. Players can be released from jail when someone touches them from their own team (who is not in jail). The jail is placed inside the opponents' territory, but within 10-15 paces of the middle line, usually marked off with sticks. Jail can also be a length of rope, tied to an immoveable object that the people in jail have to hold on to. Players who are tagged three times in enemy territory are out of the game for good and have to sit on the middle line. There is a set time for each game, perhaps 45 mins. It's great fun, although slightly hazardous – there are many things to fall over, trip up and jab yourself with in a wood. However, people generally like it and want to play all day!

Chapter 7

Coppicing and Caretaking, Empathy and Responsible Harvesting of Shared Natural Resources

"He who grabs much, grasps little" Mexican Proverb.

Living in England for the majority of my life, I have grown up in a land of plenty. As a 'thirty something' with three children, living in the lower end of the income spectrum, food is always in the cupboard, we have a roof over our heads. There are often things we want in the shops, some of which we can, and so do, buy.

It is very difficult for us, and our children, to understand real adversity when we do not generally experience food shortages and material poverty (we may all be experiencing poverty of the heart through lack of community but that is a different matter). For example, the closest we come to experiencing hunger is the feeling of an empty stomach.

However, this is not true for all people living in the UK. Ask someone who was alive during WW2 and they will tell you stories of food shortages, rationing of almost everything. My granddad would tell me how he would chase his small ration of cheese across a cream cracker to make it last. He also told me about British Olympian gymnasts had to sew red stripes on their own vests themselves in order to compete in the 1948 Olympics, because the shops were bare and pennies very tight. Listen to some of the tales from the refugees now living in Great Britain and you will hear remarkable stories that illustrate the power, adaptability and endurance of the human being when facing real adversity.

Since colonial times, British people have 'benefited' from foods harvested from other parts of the world to supplement the calorie intake of our overpopulated country, so that now we are unable to sustain ourselves solely on the food grown in our own country. It is the same in many countries around the world. Resources are shared around the globe, well, traded around the globe, to supply those who can afford them, often leaving those that can't with less than enough to survive.

Humans are greedy by nature. It is hard for us to live frugally in a way in which we are taking only what we need from the shared resources of the planet. As a Swahili proverb states: *"Greed is never finished.*" And, like a fire, humans tend consume and consume until the fuel is gone.

Part of the problem is that many of us no longer see ourselves as part of the land around us. The education we receive leads us to believe that we are separate from the world, and from each other. Each 'thing' is separate from another 'thing'. We no longer see the spirit in all things, or the interconnections and synergy of the world. We no longer have Kanyini, (as the Australian elder Bob Randall so wonderfully explains in his film of the same name). Kanyini is 'unconditional love with responsibility for all life forms'. In a nutshell, to quote Bob Randall Kanyini principles are;

"Love everybody including plants and animals. Start with your partner – love unconditionally. Extend your family to everything that's around you. Everything is vitally important. Choose 'ours' not 'mine'. Love it as 'ours'. It only develops if you do it."

When we understand that *we are what we see,* we begin to understand the need for caretaking and sharing the world's natural resources on a global scale. We then have feeling for other 'parts' of nature and a knowing that everything we do effects all our relations.

When we are out and about in the woods we can take care and be respectful, both of our own bodies and everybody else's, be it someone from the nettle, bird or fungi tribe!

How do we impart this feeling to the children and grown-ups we are with in the woods? It is no good just telling someone how to act, as the information doesn't usually get lodged in the heart but stays, if you are lucky, in the head! How are we to grow to live in a way that shares the resources on the planet and doesn't simply grab it all for one species? Some of the activities in this book, like the harvesting of materials for knife work and foraging, provide a few focussed ways to develop this attitude, working within the whole bundle of skills and activities this book provides. It is up to you, to embody this attitude, and pass it on. Anyway, before we move on to our common future, let's have a little look at the past.

Coppicing – a little history

Coppicing, as mentioned earlier, has been a traditional method of woodland management for over 5000 years. Oliver Rackham, historian of the British countryside, estimates 90% of remaining British woodland was coppiced at some stage in this most recent post glacial era.

Young tree stems are cut down to near ground level to form a 'stam' or 'stool', from which new shoots then emerge. These can be harvested again and again. Depending on the tree and the kinds of resources needed, the coppicing cycles will vary from 1 year to more than 12. Coppicing effectively keeps the tree at a young stage in its growth pattern.

In southern Britain, coppice was traditionally hazel, hornbeam, beech, ash or oak, grown amongst oak or less occasionally ash or beech standards (fully grown adult trees). In wet areas, willow and alder were coppiced. The wood these coppices provided was used for house building, fence materials, to making charcoal, hurdles, thatching materials, furniture and provided raw materials for many other crafts.

In a traditional copse, areas are cut in rotation, so there is a continuous clearing in the canopy that simulates natural clearings created by old grandfather trees falling. Such clearings, surrounded by coppice of various ages and crowned by tall standard trees, are more bio-diverse than a uniform wood with continuous canopy. Like an open heart, warmth and energy flows from the clearings, nurturing wild flowers and wild beasts. Coppicing is one way in which humans can work with nature and not against.

Coppicing was once a widespread activity, and the produce so valuable, that during medieval times, coppice workers were fined by 'verderers' if they didn't fence their coppices and protect them from the economically devastating nibblings of deer. Now only small numbers of working coppices remain, usually maintained by conservation organisations for their wildlife, aesthetic and historical value. The only remaining large-scale commercial coppice in Southern Britain is the sweet chestnut grown in Kent and East Sussex. Much of this was established as plantations in the 19th century for hop-pole production (to make barrels of mind calming beer for the rebellious masses), and is nowadays cut on a 12-18 year cycle for splitting and binding into chestnut paling fencing, fencing, or on a 20-35yr cycle for cleft post and rail fencing, or sawing into small lengths to be finger-jointed for architectural use. Other material goes to make farm fencing and to be chipped for modern wood fired heating systems. In order to continue to run a viable business, many coppices, like Powderham Woods in East Sussex, are diversifying into running bushcraft and survival skills courses, teaching traditional crafts, running forest schools and outdoor play provision. Much of the knowledge of the experienced coppice worker is being lost, but thankfully not all! The little chair on the right is being repaired with sweet chestnut bark strips at a newly planted copse in Cornwall, Pentiddy Woods.

Modern pressures

As I write, in the spring of 2009, prices of firewood, another coppicing product, look set to rise dramatically in response to the increasing prices of non-renewable fuels. Larger woodlands, managed until very recent times past as whole interdependent systems, are being split up and sold for a fast buck, as the amenity value of woodland soars, at best fragmenting the caretaking and management the whole wood,, leaving the health of woodlands and the survival of their wildlife to chance. These pressures, combined with the fact that England nowadays is one of the least wooded countries in Europe, mean that the sustainable management of woodlands is of great importance and I suggest that we should all be planting trees, not necessarily for ourselves, but for our children, and our children's children! Why not offset your annual carbon emissions by planting a few trees here in England?

The teachings of the copse

Caretaking is a mind-set that comes from being in close respectful relationship with the land and the spirit of place. The intention of caretakers is to bring the habitat(s) they are working with into natural balance, to be Nature's helping-hand, and bring about change for the greater good of all creatures living there, in a shorter timeframe than if the place was left to its own devices. It's a bit like predators naturally going for the weak, dim-witted and the old; or pests and diseases targeting the over-abundant – these are all totally natural processes that encourage a species to be stronger and fitter. 'Coppicing is not natural' you might say. Are we not *part of* nature? And surely early humans will have learnt to coppice by watching deer?

Oak leaves and lichens on the floor of a copse in Dorset.

By coppicing, with the inherent responsible and sustainable manner required for the craft, we can learn a lot about, and naturally develop a Caretaking attitude. Children are naturally caretakers, and the attitude only needs to be encouraged to develop. Coppicing involves a whole range of activities, from felling trees to creating habitat piles - coppicing appeals to natural human desires; to be destructive with one stroke and nurturing with the next. The new shoots need protecting, the produce harvested carefully with sharp tools and precise cuts to stop rot and disease getting in. Coppicing is a simple, natural metaphor for sustainable living. Planting a few willow, hazel or ash whips in your garden and maintaining them as a

148

mini copse can provide you with lots of things. You could also do a bit of guerrilla gardening and sneak out in the dead of night, armed with, say, a cherry tree or a fruit bush and a spade, to surreptitiously plant said fruiting plant as a welcome wayside snack for human and non-human travellers alike!

Finally, if you haven't experienced a copse, I recommend you go on an adventure to one near you, or perhaps visit www.smallwoods.org / www.coppiceapprentice.org.uk http://www.westcountrycoppice.co.uk/ for more information about a working copse nearby.

We made these French arrows with willow and hazel we coppiced for the spear throwing competition.

Chapter 8

Bring on the Bards! Activities to encourage the bardic voice

The word *bard* is said to have its roots in an Indo-European language where it means to *raise the voice, to praise.* In the British Isles Bards were those who sang of heroic deeds, told poems of gallant knights and strummed lutes from smoky galleries as kings feasted. They were also often, crucially, the keepers of community laws and wisdom.

Shakespeare has become synonymous with the word 'Bard'. If we are to believe the particle physicists, we all have some elementary particles inside our bodies that were once a part of the great bard's own body. We all, therefore, have a little bardic voice within us that can be encouraged to speak clearly, sing a song, bang a drum or tell a story round a camp fire. Some say a good draught of fine ale will loosen a person's tongue, however, often all that is needed is a few props to get the story going!

Storytelling is a wonderful way to develop listening skills, and imaginations. When combined with a bit of acting out, and opportunities for making props and being inspired by the landscape (micro or macro) and scenery, magic occurs. Stories seem to come from the land like flowers. People who may clam up in formal situations are moved to freely spin tales about a character they have just created from the mud beneath their feet. People gather and listen as a song flows, and join together in the pulse and beat of dancing feet and a clapping of hands. According to Jay Griffiths, in her book about time, *Pip Pip*, the communities of England had a great number of stories and music, coming together in the form of festivals, that celebrated the land, its features, and its cycles. Since the enclosures, 200 years or so ago, they have all but died out. Something within the spirit of the community died when the land became fenced off from the commoner. So let's get out there and make up stories, sing songs, dance and have little festivals whenever we can!

Dancing on Dartmoor to the sound of the Didgeridoo!

Blobster heroes and tales of great deeds!

What follows is a couple of activities to encourage story telling, story re-telling or writing, depending on the outcomes you desire. These activities encourage stories to emerge from the landscape. There is a word-rhythm activity too. The song of the land rises once more! All I will deal with is the outdoor, how-to stuff, and leave the pens and paper to you, if you so desire.

Storylines
Ages 4-104
Group size: 30 or less
Up to an hour

Ready

This is a simple adventure story-making activity using a piece of string and natural objects. Remind participants of the Australian Aboriginal songlines, and perhaps point out some of the local environmental features, making up pretend names and little stories about what happened where. This will engage the storymakers, as will asking them about their favourite characters in stories they know, so spend a few minutes setting up the activity with a circle time involving everybody.

Get set

You will need a ball of string or some rope that drapes and runs along the surface of the terrain you are playing in. Cut it into lengths. How long a piece? Well, that's up to you! But at least a pace or two, no more than 10. Perhaps some clay to make blobsters with.

The activity works equally well with people making up stories individually, in pairs or small groups, but does ideally need a ratio of one teacher/mentor to a maximum of five participants to make sure everyone has the opportunity to tell their story.

Go!

"Here is your string. Lay it out on the ground. Make sure the string goes over or through some interesting natural features...logs, twigs, a stream, a pebble or rock, grass, pine needles etc (remember that where the string lies is shared by many other living organisms). One end of the string is the beginning of the story. Creatures and objects along and under the string can become a part of your story."

"Stand at one end of the string. Visualise the spirits inside everything around you. Have a little look around for a small object or two that you can pretend is a creature or a person - stones, pine cones, a bit of clay, interesting knobbly bits of wood, seed pods etc. If you like, add natural legs/eyes/ hair/tails/tools or weapons. Hey presto, you have a character or two ready for an adventure. And you can pretend to be anything you want to be. (If you can't find anything wild to be, you can pretend to be anyone you want to be...Luke Skywalker, a Pokemon...)"

"Off you go down the string, and the story begins to tell itself as your imagination is inspired by the journey of your character along the story line".

Children usually have great imaginations and it doesn't take long before there are all kinds of problems to overcome, friends and foe to meet, deeds to do and places to rest presenting themselves along the way. Some even crawl out of the woodwork! Literally.

"As the story develops, let your instinct for creation come out too! Start adding to what is there, making mini bridges, pretend fires, caves, grottos, castles, meet dragons, hairy bunyips in billabongs..."

Some brave blobsters travelling across a grassy plain – the rope is in the top left of the photo.

After 15-20 mins of story-making call everyone in.

"OK. Finish off your stories within the next minute and come on in! We are going to share our stories in small groups now. Get into groups of up to 5 in each group please. Decide who is going to go first, then go to their storyline and listen to the story. No interrupting please! When each person has finished, give a little round of applause and move on to the next person, until you are all done."

Useful things to know.

It is fascinating to note what kinds of characters the players want to be, and sometimes insightful too! There are many ways to extend and adapt the activity. You can:

- Suggest a starting line for the story: "One day I went into the woods. I hadn't gone far when I heard a ... "
- Focus the story-making by suggesting a theme, like turning it into a quest for example. Quests involve the hero or heroine going off on an adventure and coming back changed in some way. Other themes include numbers (three bridges to cross, three heroes, three beasts etc), monsters, mythical beasts, wizards and witches, deception, Good Samaritans, and so on.
- Ask the storytellers to stop at the end of their string with a cliff-hanger. They then pair up, and once they have all told their stories, the tellers swop storylines, and make up their version of what happens next to continue their partner's story.
- Introduce a dilemma or two, simple survival issues like "what if all the water runs out, how would the characters get something to

drink?", or "the characters need somewhere to stay overnight, what shall we do?".

- The activity can be based around issues like going for a picnic, overcoming problems, getting lost. The older the storytellers the deeper the issues: inner conflict, war, sharing resources, peak oil and transport, town planning!
- Make the string into a circle, so the story becomes a cycle. You can then introduce concepts of cycles in nature, life cycles etc.
-

I hope you have fun!

How did you get here?
4-104
Group size: 30 or less
About and hour

Ready

This activity can be played simply for fun in the mythical and magical realm, or it can be used for getting to know each other, when a group is going to be spending a lot of time with each other for example. So, in this case, even if the stories of 'how did you get here?' *are* personal, most of the time people will only share what they want to share about their own life journey. (In rare cases, when members of the group trust one another, there is a chance that someone will disclose sensitive information, which is something you need to prepared for, just in case.)

"So, how did you get to the top of this hill, Steve?". "Well, my hair was a lot shorter when I set off. It wasn't white either. It turned white the day I…"

Get set

As for the activity above, except you will also need enough small bags of trail mix for each group to have one to share.

Go!

The class is primed by telling them a little about bards, and the epic journey tales they would tell. The scene is set by talking about the times when there were fairies, dragons and knights, bridges with trolls and swamps full of hissing snakes.

"Today we are going to be making up stories of 'how we got here'. Imagine you're a traveller and you meet a few other travellers at a crossroads one evening. You decide to make a fire together, sit down, bring out food to share from your bags, cook dinner and then tell each other the stories of what happened on the way to the cross roads"

"I would like each of you to make some kind of blobster – be it a knight, a princess, a Jedi, a goblin, a hedgehog or an orphan football star..."

When we are all ready, or as individuals become ready – (you choose) divide the class into groups of four(ish). Each group has to choose a place as a pretend crossroads, and make a small pretend fire, then to come back when they have finished.

"What do we do now?"

"Find a stick that is as tall as you are. Place your sticks with one end pointing to your pretend fire, and the other end pointing out from the fire. Place your blobster at the end of the stick, farthest away from the fire. That is the start of your story. Now make up an adventure story of your blobster's journey and how it came to meet the other travellers at the crossroads. At this point, the story you are making up is just for you. You will share it later. If you want to you can build things along the stick, to become parts of your story... There may be fire breathing salamanders, mountains, endless plains of grass, witches with bottomless cauldrons, football matches with giants, and other fantastical happenings and magical creatures along the way... its up to you. Have fun. When you have all finished making up your story, come back here."

Eventually they come back with, "What do we do now?"

"Take this bag of trail mix, go back to your fireplace, share the feast, and take it in turns to tell or act out your blobsters' adventure story. Your blobster can act it all out if you like, and make sound effects!"

Useful things to know

When everyone is done, you can test listening skills and extend the activity by asking everybody to remember the story they liked most from their group, and show and tell it to someone from another group, using the good old "Once upon a time there was a..."

It is also possible to extend this activity by placing another long stick on the ground, facing out from the fire, using it to guide and inspire the story of a band of travellers setting off on a quest, with beasts to tame and, problems to solve and difficulties to overcome!

When all is said and done, you are left with a lovely collection of 'storyboard' temporary environmental art sculptures. Not bad for an hour's play!

Name-drumming layer cake!
Age 7-107
Group size: up to 30
25 mins

The first time I tried it with a group they got really into it and spontaneously introduced mouth noises. The noise changed from hums to yelps and the whole group joined in and followed the rest. The teacher and I had real trouble working out who was instigating the changes but I think it was different people. There was a really rare feeling of oneness around our fire for about 10 minutes. Magic.
Richard Irvine, Devon Discovery

Ready

Setting up a drumming circle can be a noisy and fun experience. A name-drumming orchestra is a simple way to start drumming in big groups. Once a basic stomping rhythm has been established, the players can use their own names to play their part of the over-all rhythm. You can use the names of plants or animals or descriptive words instead of human names if you like.

Get set

You will need two short sturdy sticks that you can hit together without them breaking (although, if you need a cheap gag... have one that *will* break, and a spare one as back up). Choose a suitable spot to gather the group in a circle (I usually do this activity standing in a circle, but you can always do it around a circle of logs or along a fallen tree trunk). Trying to explain how to drum using the written word has been challenging, so bear with me, and hopefully you will have enough understanding to give it a go!

A useful thing to know

If you find it hard to stomp, count and hit out your name pattern all at once, while pointing to the players in turn (as I do!!!), you can ask someone to step in to the middle of the circle to be the conductor. Basically, the role of the conductor is to keep the beat steady and point to people. The conductor counts "1, 2, 1, 2..." along with the stomps and then, when the rhythm is steady, points to each person in turn (about every four "1, 2s"). If you are already confused and there are too many ones and twos...take a breath and read on!

Go!

"Okay everybody! We're going to have some drumming practice! We are going to make a layer cake of sound by drumming our names. Please go and find two sticks you can hit together, that sound good, like this!"
I demonstrate hitting the sticks together.

"Okay, off you go, and when you've found your sticks come right back here!" When everyone is returns, we form a circle and I demonstrate hitting out the rhythm, or pattern, of my name:

"Chris-to-pher Holl-and", with three short, and two long beats - one for each syllable of my name. (Another way to do it would be to do three soft and two loud.) I get everyone to copy my name pattern a couple of times, in a call and response way.

We then work slowly round the circle with each person hitting out their name pattern and it being repeated by the rest of the group. There will be a few sticks that break mid performance and this can be the cause of much hilarity. Laughter is good. It creates timeless bonds between people, and the place.

"Right! In a moment we'll begin with one name pattern being hit-out repeatedly, and then slowly, a name at a time, build our layer cake of sound until we are all drumming our names together. Then we will slowly stop drumming, one person at a time, until there is silence, and we can watch the last ripple of sound flow out across the land!"

"But first, we need to start with a pulse, an even beat to keep us in rhythm." Now start a slow walking-on-the-spot pulse, (about one beat per second is fine) and encourage everybody to join in:

"stomp....stomp....stomp....stomp...."
I mentally count "1, 2, 1, 2..." along with the stomps.

Then begin to add name patterns to the stomping pulse by either choosing someone to go first or simply by starting with my own name. After every 1,2,1,2, cycle point to the next person, so that each player adds their name pattern to the layer cake, and so that it fits in with the rhythm, like this for example:

Stomp,	stomp,		stomp,	stomp,	
1	2		1	2	
chris-to-pher	holl-	and,	chris-to-pher	holl-	and,
to-	ny	hunt,	to-	ny	hunt,

Slowly a wonderful polyrhythmic, sometimes cacophonic orchestra builds to a crescendo layer cake of sound! Hold it there for a while and bathe in the bliss of the noise before slowly pointing to everyone in turn again, and slowly each person stops drumming their name pattern, until only silence remains, and the last concentric ring of sound spreads out across the land like a ripple across a pond. Imagine it going, going, going...with stillness following like a calm breath. At this point, crouch down, pointing to the ground, with arms out low and wide to signify silence....

Waiting... Mimicking the sound rippling off into the land...

Waiting...   And when ready, after a theatrical pause, (with everybody watching me), I whisper "Final drum roll!"

Slowly we stand up, raising hands above heads, clicking our sticks as we go. Everyone does a final drum-roll together, and then   finish the finale by, jumping up and cutting the air in a flourish to finish!

Chapter 9

Wild First Aid

This chapter is not about how to cope with worst-case first aid situations in the woods, where you have only a handkerchief, a ripe banana and a few coins to deal with an emergency. In this chapter, I do three things:

- Suggest that there is great merit, for people of all ages, in knowing how they can respond to some of the first aid situations most likely to occur outdoors.
- Provide you, the first aider, with a fun way to refresh yourself with best practice in a first aid situation, while giving your charges opportunities to play at being a first aider.
- Inform you about a few common wild plants you might find useful in minor first aid situations, and give you an example of a more 'holistic' first aid kit. The ABCDE of first aid is Airways, Breathing, Circulation, Deformities and Emotions, and alternative first aid remedies act on the body, mind and the heart.

Initial responses count

I was amazed and proud of my 8yr old daughter's behaviour recently when the tip of an escaping whittling knife made a deep hole in my thigh when I was packing kit into the car for a camp. I came into the house white faced, holding the outside of my left leg. She looked on in interest as I cleaned the wound and applied some steri-strips. Ok, she did go "euuuuw" and look away for a moment, but she was soon looking back to see what I was doing. When I had cleaned myself up I lay on the couch, with my leg up, applying more pressure to the wound. She took herself off into the kitchen and made me a cup of sweet tea! Without any prompting!

"That is a perfect first aid response," I told her gratefully.

Being able to keep calm in adverse situations comes from a lack of fear. Simply, first aid is about making sure the injured person's condition isn't getting any worse, calling for help, and keeping the injured person alive until the experts arrive. In first aid situations, some people are naturally fearless and simply respond to a situation with great common sense and practicality.

Others are left in a dither, running round in circles like headless chickens, too panicked or not knowing how to respond. Experience is often the key to overcoming the fear that arises in such situations. So, it is good for people to have some experience of problematic situations, and to know how, and when they can make a real difference to someone in difficulty.

However, over-confidence (too much fearlessness) can sometimes lead to someone taking unacceptable risks and being the *cause* of a first aid situation! Again, it is experience that develops a sense of what is, and what is not an acceptable risk.

Wet logs are more slippery than dry ones, but there is seldom any use in telling a young person that information; it's better to allow them to find out for themselves, in a 'safe' environment. A safe environment does not mean it is entirely risk free! It is our responsibility as parents, leaders and educators to put our children in a place of acceptable risk so that they can learn from situations and build up the neurological pathways needed to facilitate the healthy development of the whole person. Children like to put themselves in new and sometimes dangerous situations because adversity nurtures resourcefulness. This is why children test our boundaries so much – they want to learn. They are hungry for experience.

Take tree climbing for an example - a brilliant activity for developing strength, stamina, judgment of distances, hand-eye co-ordination, moving in different ways and planes. It's something almost every small person will want to try. Risky? Yes, of course, and the higher you climb, the harder you fall. How risky? While reading the spring 2009 National Trust magazine I read that research has shown that more children are admitted to hospital from injuries sustained from falling out of bed that falling out of trees! The only way someone can become a better climber is through extending his or her experience. By climbing a different shape of tree, or gaining greater heights, new skills can be developed. By playing in different species of trees, the climbers learn about the qualities and strengths of wood in various tree species. Slowly but surely, through experience, the climber becomes more adept at assessing the risks of a wide range of tree climbing situations, and there is less and less risk of that person falling from the tree they are climbing.

However, accidents do happen. What if someone falls from a tree while in your care? Perhaps a group of friends are in the woods around a campsite you are staying at. They are climbing trees. One of them doesn't notice a dead branch and falls 20ft face down to the ground, unconscious, with a broken back. How the friends respond in the next few minutes could affect the rest of their mate's life. Knowing what to do in that kind of situation is useful learning, possibly more useful than remembering the names of Egyptian Gods or pi to three decimal places!

So, how can we provide the learning required to respond effectively in a first aid situation, without the risk?

Role-play is a wonderful way to provide experience without anyone really being hurt. It is easy to think up possible situations, write them down on a scrap of paper, put them all in a hat and hand them out to small groups to enact and come up with good practical ideas of "what you could do if..." It can be fun to wrap someone up in a bandage, tie a splint to an arm, make a stretcher, or hop around screaming, pretending you have just poured boiling hot water on your leg! As well as having a laugh, learning how to respond to simple first aid incidents and accidents can be a source of great self-esteem to some people. It also helps us feel more confident about being in the great outdoors when we are equipped with an idea of "what to do if". Being more confident will hopefully mean that a person also feels more at home and relaxed in nature.

Useful things to know

If you want to find out more about what to do in a certain kind of first aid situation there is plenty of help on the web, just type in 'first aid' and you will find there are many pages of information from the St John's Ambulance, the BBC, the Red Cross etc. There are also many first aid courses available, but not all deal with practical first aid in 'wilder' settings. For outdoor first aid expertise, there is Devon Discovery, Wilderness First Aid and Rubicon Solutions, all of whom have websites with details of their training courses. On a final note, I trained, and now refresh regularly with Devon Discovery and going back to role play, had a lot of fun learning some valuable lessons, in pretend situations, up on Dartmoor. But that is another story for round the campfire...

Wild first aid role-play.
Ages 7 and over
About an hour for a group of 16, 4 teams of 4

Ready
You will need pens, paper, a hat or two, first aid kit, parcel tape, perhaps some roll mats to lie on or to use as splints.

Get Set
Set the scene. Explain what First Aid is. Perhaps you could ask if anyone in the group has had direct experience of needing or giving first aid before. Open the topic of risk assessment. Find out what kinds of activities are considered dangerous or risky, and ask the group to come up with some scenarios in which something dangerous happens, and someone or some people get hurt. Write down some of the scenarios.

Go!
Pop all the scenarios into a hat. Divide your group into smaller teams, get each team to choose a scenario and go away and prepare to act it out in their own way. Remind everyone to freeze-frame at the moment of the 'accident', so that the audience can come up with their own ideas of 'what happens next'.

As a facilitator wearing a 'first-aider' hat, it is your job to ensure that each group comes up with some kind of suitable first aid response to finish the role play so everyone can live happily ever after, so to speak.

Natural first aid kit

It seems that most of the occasions that require me to reach for the first aid kit are for cuts, bruises, burns, bites and stings. There are also times when people have headaches and upset tummies and a basic herbal first aid kit can help tremendously with such cases.

The following four plants constitute a mini medicine chest. An interesting fact about each plant follows the first aid descriptions as another 'aide memoire'.

Greater Plantain, *Plantago major,* broadleaved plantain, Soldiers herb, white man's footsteps. I use this common herb, (or weed as some would call it!) in several ways:

- **To stop bleeding** Several young leaves, chewed up briefly and applied to a bleeding cut or wound as a compress, will aid coagulation in moments. Another leaf over the top will keep the compress in place! This is how it earned its name of 'soldiers herb'.

- **To ease diarrhoea** The whole plant can be washed, chopped up finely, and then eaten to relieve the condition.
- **Splinters and thorns** Placing some warm, chewed up leaves on splinters and thorns can help draw them out.
- **Bites and stings** The chewed up leaves placed on insect stings and bites will relieve pain. It is said that plantain roots are effective against rattlesnake bites, but I haven't needed to try that one yet!
- **Toothache** Placing a wad of chewed leaves at the base of a sore tooth can help reduce the pain.
- **Insect repellent** The seeds are very rich in b vitamins, so help keep insects away, however, lemon balm leaves rubbed on are more immediately effective.

Plantago major earned the name 'white man's footsteps' from the way it spreads its seeds. Early settlers to the northern American continent brought the plant with them. As they walked about, the plantain seeds, which travel about in the shoes, hooves, and claws of walking animals, followed the white man as he travelled about in the red man's land.

Yarrow, *Achillea millefolium* The first aid applications of yarrow are:

- **To stop bleeding** Several leaves, chewed up briefly and applied to a bleeding cut or wound as a compress, will aid coagulation in moments.
- **Appetite and Digestive stimulant** Several leaves, made into a tea or chewed and then swallowed can help with the loss of appetite, and stimulate a sluggish digestion
- **Toothache** Placing a wad of chewed leaves at the base of a sore tooth can help reduce the pain.
- **Fevers and colds**   Yarrow is a number one fever herb, and a good tonic for colds when made into a strong herbal tea. Make a pot and drink a cupful every few hours to help sweat out a fever or cold.

Roman legionaries, who marched a long way, stuffed *Achillea millefolium* into their sandals to help stop the bleeding.

Elder, *Sambucus nigra.* **Elder** is often described as the complete medicine chest. Here are some of the reasons why:

- **Anticatarrhal and expectorant** The flowers make a lovely tea, especially when combined with lemon juice, for fevers, influenza and catarrhal conditions of the upper respiratory tract and lungs. It encourages sweating, the removal of phlegm and is anti-inflammatory.
- **Mouthwash** The warm or cold tea from the flowers makes a soothing mouthwash and gargle for sore throats, mouth ulcers and tonsillitis
- **Eyewash** elderflower tea, well strained and cooled, makes an excellent eyewash for eyes that are sore and inflamed from too much wood smoke.
- **Insect repellent** Rubbing the leaves on exposed parts of the body can keep insects at bay. Sadly not midges though!
- **Sprains and bruises** The leaves, scrunched up first to break some of the cell walls, can be rubbed on or applied as a compress to sprains and bruises.

- **Laxative** The flowers, and more so the berries, are laxative, so help when someone is a constipated. The bark is purgative and can be used in extreme circumstance to get things going!
- **Hayfever.** The flowers, fresh from the bushes, make a preventative tea for hayfever sufferers before the pollen count rises too high. The dried flowers combined with peppermint, yarrow and boneset make a tea to help hayfever sufferers with red eyes and loads of snot!

Elderflower heads, dipped in a light batter, briefly fried and sprinkled with sugar make a lovely wayside sweet treat.

Sunset behind an elder in a hedge.

There are also a few other plants really worth knowing about. Dock leaves are useful to help stop nettle stings. Burdock leaves can be chewed (very bitter!) and applied for effective relief of bee stings. Pine needles, when boiled for a few minutes and allowed to stand make a disinfectant solution. Lavender flowers and chamomile flowers, when rubbed and sniffed ease nervous headaches. Crushed daisy flowers can help with bruises and sprains. When employing the help of plant medicines it is always wise to give thanks for their help, as the following story from my life shows, there is more to a plant than its' chemical composition.

Plant spirits to the rescue

Occasionally something happens out of the blue that changes your mind about how the world works. On this occasion, first aid came from a truly wild, and for me, unexpected source. One day, while travelling in Australia, I was in desperate need of some first aid on my forearm. I was mowing someone's garden with a heavy, old, rotary mower.

As I was negotiating a sloping lawn round a rocky herb bed, the blade must have jammed on an immovable rock. The mower suddenly jerked forwards, pulling me right off my feet! My right forearm felt as if it had been ripped open. Looking at it, I could see there was no damage on the surface, but something really wrong had happened on the inside. I was a streaming torrent of antipodean vernacular. Looking around me for some help, I saw a rosemary bush. Rosemary essential oil is good for sprains and muscular aches, so I spoke to the plant, thanking it for its healing qualities, picked a sprig, and scrunched it up a little in my fist, before rubbing it on my right arm. I was expecting the oil to take effect in some minutes, but my arm stopped hurting completely, and immediately!

Wow! How could that happen? Oils were supposed to soak into the skin before the chemistry started to work...in time I settled with the belief that the rosemary plant spirit had jumped into action at my call for help and saved the day, and my perspective on the unseen elements to the world shifted accordingly.

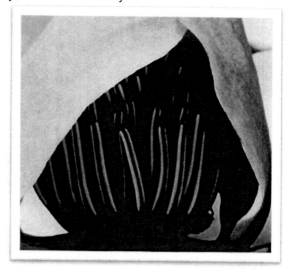

It wasn't until a few years later that I came upon a book by Elliot Cowan called *Plant Spirit Medicine* outlining a whole school of shamanic medicine involving plant spirits that goes back thousands of years. The plant spirits are there, and they have medicine. Not necessarily for cuts and bruises, but certainly for healing of the whole person - mentally, physically, spiritually.

Second Aid Kit

For your interest, here is a list of complementary first aid items I carry in my kit, alongside the usual plasters, bandages, steri-strips, tweezers, tick remover, paracetamol, etc, in case the plants I have mentioned above are not readily available. I hope you find it useful.

In this day of health and safety paranoia and litigation, I find it necessary to get the participants' permission to use the following:

- Lavender essential oil
- Melissa (comp) tincture
- Olbas Oil
- Ginger sweets or crystallised ginger
- Arnica 30 pillules
- Tea tree essential oil
- Propolis tincture

Lavender essential oil is basically an all-in-one medicine chest, so it can be used in many situations. (It has many medicinal properties including: antiseptic, analgesic, anti-convulsant, anti-depressant, anti-rheumatic, anti-spasmodic, anti-inflammatory, antiviral, bactericide, carminative, cholagogue, cordial, decongestant, deodorant, diuretic, emmenagogue, hypotensive, nervine, rubefacient, sedative, sudorific and vulnerary.) It can be applied directly onto the skin of most people so can be used neat in most cases. How can it be used? Here's a list of how I most commonly use it:
- On bites and stings to relieve pain and itching
- On cuts and grazes as an antiseptic
- On minor burns and sunburn
- Rubbed into the scalp and forehead for headaches
- Dropped onto a cloth or clothing to be sniffed, relieving anxiety, panic, tension and insomnia
- Rubbed on skin to repel some biting insects (not midges!)
- To relieve irritating coughs when used in a steam inhalation

Melissa tincture is a mixture of tinctures, with the main ingredient being Melissa, or lemon balm. This tincture, made by Weleda, is simply the best solution for the kind of upset tummy where someone is feeling nauseous - usually from some kind of nervous of mental disposition, the kind of thing that happens on someone's first trip to the woods, away from parents or familiar surroundings.

Olbas oil, a mixture of essential oils, is used as a decongesting inhalant, and a muscle rub for aches and sprains. It can also be used for relief of bites and stings.

Ginger sweets are for helping with travel sickness and nausea, as well as internally getting the heat going in someone who is cold or getting towards hypothermic.

Arnica is used for bruises and sprains, as well as shock and helping to stop bleeding.

Tea tree essential oil is one of the most powerful natural antiseptics, as well as being antiviral, antibacterial and antifungal. It can be used neat on many people's skins, but is sometimes even more effective at a 2% dilution in water. It is used for cleaning wounds, as an inhalant for colds, on athletes' foot, against herpes simplex (cold sores) and generally improving both emotional wellbeing and immuno-repsonse to disease.

Propolis tincture the best thing to apply to a puncture wound caused by a blackthorn spine. It is the most effective substance to deal with the nasty infections that can be caused by the really small algae and lichens living on the spines. It can be applied directly to cuts and grazes to keep the wound infection free, and taken internally, neat or with water, juice or honey, for sore throats, coughs and colds.

However, this is a list of what I personally keep in my medicine bag, and you will no doubt have your own favourite essentials. I do recommend, though, that you get to know some of the first aid plants, especially, plantain, yarrow, elder, and I suggest you always carry a bottle of lavender essential oil!

Chapter 10

Making the Links and Joined Up Thinking

This chapter is about physically joining things together in the world, and how the metaphor of weaving and tying can help us link into the web of life in a real and practical way.

Seeing the links between disparate objects and events can be very difficult these days. The world we live in, and are part of, has become very 'large'. We are no longer living in small clans or village communities that provide us with everything we need to survive. For most of us who read this book the 'things' we have in our everyday lives are sourced from all over the globe and not from our immediate surroundings, as they were a few hundred years ago, and so the effects of our actions are not so easily noticed. For example, when we buy a book it may have been printed and bound on the other side of the planet from the original timber from which it was made and which might have been logged a thousand miles away from the printing press, and the printing might have used inks made from GM soya beans in yet another part of the world. The energy used to print and transport this book to you may have come from fossil fuels or renewable energy, and whichever it is, there will be a whole gamut of effects on the environment, locally and globally.

It is very difficult to see the actual effects of the consumer choices we make. By encouraging joined up thinking, we encourage our children to see the world as a plethora of interwoven systems, not a bunch of objects and events isolated in time and space. We can encourage inquisitiveness by tugging on a strand of the web of life and asking what happens if I do 'this'.

For example, let's consider a lime tree, *Tilia cordata*, for example. A tree is just a tree? No, it is an ecosystem, providing habitat and food for a whole host of organisms from bacteria to birds. How could a tree such as a lime tree have affected humans? Surely it is a separate object, and if we have no reason to have a relationship with the plant now what has it got to do with us? What are the links?

There may be a clue in the name *cordata* - lime trees make excellent cordage! By making string from the plant, we begin to see how the strands of circumstance relate to our lives. The inner bark, or bast, has been used by humans for thousands of years to make string and rope of many thicknesses. It could be that some lime-bark cordage was used to bind the fletchings of an arrow one of your ancestors used to kill a deer that sustained her through one tough winter. Without that meat and hide she would have died, and you wouldn't be here now. Perhaps one of your ancestors made a raft of wood lashed together with lime bark rope, and that raft made it to the island your other ancestors lived on. It may be that now you drink some kind of relaxing herb tea, with linden blossom in it (*Tilia* species blossom), to help your mind unwind from business so you can sleep peacefully and therefore cope with the next day. Perhaps the honey you eat is partially made from nectar that bees have collected from Tilia trees. Who knows how many links you have with a lime tree, past and present. If you start tugging at the web of life, you will soon see that all things are connected...

Stephen Harold Buhner is an ecologist who has been studying the effects of the medicines we humans use to heal ourselves on the environments we live in. In his brilliant book, which I recommend reading, on the ecological importance of plants and plant medicines to life on earth, *The Lost Language of Plants*, he reveals some of the incredible ways natural systems are affected by the chemicals we, and other organisms, produce. Buhner suggests human kind is at a very interesting point in its history in that we are making so many profound and invisible changes that we cannot possibly keep track of them. We are loosing the thread, so speak, of the effects we have on the world around us.

Cordage, be it a sewing thread or a thick mooring rope for ocean liners, is made from many separate fibres, all wound together to produce a cord, turning a chaotic bundle of fibres into a yarn made up of plies, twisted round and round each other. DNA (Deoxyribonucleic acid), is a double helix made from simple chemical elements wound round and round each other. Up close, it looks like a two-ply yarn. DNA makes up hereditary material present in the nucleus of cells, the building blocks of all living organisms.

Humans all over the world, for thousands of years, have made cordage. Cordage making was one of the first craft processes to be industrialised, and cloth making was a significant driving force in the industrial revolution and subsequently the way the first computers were designed. We humans would not be who we are today without this ability to turn the 'chaos' of nature into all kinds of clothes, chemicals, and machines. It may be that our ability to turn nature into order might, in turn, spin our civilisations back into chaos.

Making cordage by hand involves repetitive movements of fingers and hands. Some people say crafts involving repetitive movements with both hands develop links between the left and right hemispheres of the brain, and strengthens the myelin sheath. The myelin sheath is an insulating material essential to proper functioning of the nervous system in vertebrates (animals with backbones), and it helps signals travelling along axioms, (a very long thin kind of nerve cells), to stay on track as they weave through the nervous system. This in turn helps with the deliberate, ordered movement required to operate a large body with many moving parts.

Weaving the walls of an 'African' hut.

Repetitive crafts like cordage making, spinning and knitting seem to bring order to the psyche too. Many people will tell you it makes them feel peaceful and relaxed. While teaching, I have noticed that once people have learnt how to make cordage or weave willow, a peaceful atmosphere permeates the camp, with people quietly nattering away to each other. It is also said that knitting is the new yoga!

All the remaining tribal groups, which have needed an incredible internal, flexible order in their communities to survive the 'guns, germs and steel' of industrialised cultures, have strong cordage and basket-making traditions. Making baskets and string enables people to sit and chat. Time spent with others in this 'crafty' way binds communities together just like the interwoven strands in a basket. I would argue that we westerners really benefit from picking up some simple crafts to rekindle our own community spirit.

Knot work in art and jewellery, involving seemingly

endless interwoven yarns, can symbolise the interconnectedness of life. One of the simplest 'celtic' knots (more accurately Christian Saxon manuscript decorations), symbolises the interconnected and inseparable triune of mind, body and spirit, or perhaps of head, heart and hands.

Learning and teaching how to physically tie knots and lashings is one way to start the process of connecting ourselves to nature, thus joining up our thinking. It is important understand the metaphor and hold the intention of connection in your mind as you are teaching. As with healing, one of the most important parts of the process is of the intent of the healer to heal.

A true listening heart may be a more effective remedy than a pill prescribed in haste as surgery is closing. So I suggest it is important to know *why* you are teaching something, on as many levels as possible. For me, teaching knots is about weaving us in to the interconnectedness of life. It is a good opportunity to remind people of our connections with nature, and there is no better way to do this than to tell a story, (or spin a yarn:-) at the same time!

The Legend of the Dreamcatcher.

There are many versions of the Dreamcatcher legend, from different tribes across North America. The one I first came across features an elder from the Lakota people, who climbs mountain to seek a dream or vision of how to teach his children and his children's children about how all life is connected. His cry for a dream is granted when he is given a Dreamcatcher by Iktomi, the keeper of wisdom. One version of the story appears below:

Long ago when the world was young, an old Lakota spiritual leader was on a high mountain and there he had a vision. In his vision, Iktomi, the great trickster and teacher of wisdom, appeared in the form of a spider. Iktomi spoke to him in a sacred language. As he spoke, Iktomi the

spider picked up the elder's willow hoop that had feathers, horsehair, beads and offerings on it, and began to spin a web.

He spoke to the elder about the cycles of life; how we begin our lives as infants, move on through childhood and on to adulthood. Finally we go to old age where we must be taken care of as infants, completing the cycle. "But", Iktomi said as he continued to spin his web, "in each time of life there are many forces; some good and some bad. If you listen to the good forces, they will steer you in the right direction. But, if you listen to the bad forces, they'll steer you in the wrong direction and may hurt you. So these forces can either help, or can interfere, with the harmony of Nature." While the spider spoke, he continued to weave his web.

When Iktomi finished speaking, he gave the elder the web and said, "The web is a perfect circle with a hole in the center. Use the web to help your people reach their goals, making good use of their ideas, dreams and visions. If you believe in Great Spirit, the web will catch your good ideas and the bad ones will go through the hole."

The elder passed on his vision to the people and now many Indian people hang a dream catcher above their bed to sift their dreams and visions. The good is captured in the web of life and carried with the people, but the evil in their dreams drops through the hole in the centre of the web and is no longer a part of their lives.

I like to tell a version of the story, drawing on the audience for various recurring sound effects, while making a dreamcatcher from willow and yarn or string. It is important to weave the audience into the story to help with the general interconnectedness theme of this chapter. To make the hoop I use a willow 'wand' from a willow 'stool' to represent the fact it was one elder, from village or tribe, who went off to seek something for the benefit of the whole tribe.

How to make a Dreamcatcher.

A dreamcatcher is made by tying one end of a yarn to a hoop of wood, and then making a spiral of blanket stitches, from the rim of the hoop to the centre. It is that simple. Beads and feathers can be woven in along the way. If you haven't done so already, email me with your details and I will send you a link of a video of me telling the story at the Wilderness Gathering, Wiltshire, UK in 2009.

Webbing activity
Group size: up to 30
From 7 onwards
15-20 minutes

Ready
This activity is one I have picked up somewhere along the trail. I give thanks to whoever came up with the idea. It shows how one element in a system can affect the whole, and how important all the little parts of a natural system are to the functioning and stability of a natural system. I use it to show how all things are related (connected), and how the loss of one part of a web of life in one habitat affects everything else, directly or indirectly.

Get Set
You will need a ball of wool, string or yarn and to have everybody sitting in a circle.

Go!
We are gathering in a little woodland.

"Let's sit in a circle."

Choose one person to name something they can see around them. They say "A tree", for example. Give them the ball of wool and ask them to hold onto the end of the yarn. Pose a question to the rest of the group that reveals a relationship with the "thing", in this case, a tree.

For example: "What do trees need to grow?" "Soil." Comes an answer from someone.

The person who originally said, "tree" now throws the wool to the "soil" person (but still holds on to the end of the yarn!). The "soil" person takes hold of the yarn and gets ready for the next relationship-revealing question to be asked, "What else do trees need to grow?" Hopefully someone comes up with the answer "Water".

Now "soil" throws the wool to the "water" person. And so it goes on, with me asking questions that will prompt the group to give answers such as, "nutrients", for example, or ..."rotting leaves", "spiders and bugs", "birds", "people"... and so on until a whole host of relationships is revealed and/or the wool runs out!

Now is a good time to introduce the Native American concept of "All our relations". It shows a respect for the sacredness of life and a deep understanding that what we do to ourselves, we do to the web of life. To demonstrate this, we take the game through another step.

"Now, suppose we take one of the elements in our web away...say we take away all the rotting leaves on the woodland floor?" The person who came up with the "rotting leaves" answer gives the web a tug by pulling the section of yarn they are holding. Anyone who feels that tug can be seen to have a direct relationship to the "rotting leaves". The people who feel the tug then pull on their bit of yarn. Soon enough the tug is felt cross the whole circle. It is an activity people really remember and it can be done with many levels of understanding.

Knots, hitches and good ole lashing!

As you now see, there can be much more depth to the teaching of knots, hitches and lashings than you think. First, there is the reason for wanting to tie that particular knot or hitch with that particular cordage. Then consider the skills needed for making the cordage, and the skills of preparing the materials you are making the cordage from, and the knowledge needed for the harvesting and preparation of the raw materials, and the effect your harvesting has on the ecosystem it comes from, and so on.

Chris teaching lashings to forest school leaders – thanks to Laura H for the photo.

What is a **knot**? A **knot** is a method for fastening or securing linear material such as a yarn or rope by tying or interweaving. A **hitch** is used to fasten cordage to an object. A **lashing** is an arrangement of cord or rope fastening two or more objects together in a somewhat rigid fashion.

To some knots!

Figure of eight – used to stop ropes from fraying or coming undone at the end, and yet is easy to undo.

Reef knot – useful for tying together two ropes of similar thickness when you want to get the knot undone again easily.

Left over right and under.....right over left and   through...

Pull both ends with equal strength to tighten.

Fisherman's knot – used when two ropes of similar thickness need joining in a way that will not slip undone.

Clove hitch – it's a self-tightening hitch that is easily adjustable at the same time... I use it at one end of the bow I use to make fire by friction. It is also the ideal way to start a square lashing... coming up next.

Make two loops by twisting the rope in your right thumb and forefinger.

Put the second, lower loop over, the top of the first.

Pop the two loops over the end of the piece of wood you want to attach to, and pull the two ends to tighten up the hitch. Now you know the shape of the knot, have a go fastening a clove hitch directly onto the middle of a piece of wood – i.e., where you cant put the two loops over one end!

Square lashing – for fixing two pieces of wood together at 90 degrees to one another (like balance beams to trees!)

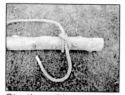  

Starting with a clove hitch on one piece of wood, then lay the other piece of wood over the first. Thread the long end over the top piece and under the bottom piece, binding under and over and a few times...

until it looks something like this...   Then wrap the long end

horizontally, 'between' the pieces of wood, thus tightening the binding you have already done.

Finish with a reef knot.

Timber hitch and killick hitch – these hitches are excellent for dragging long branches, the killick hitch is a timber hitch with extra bit!

Start like this, then loop the right hand bit of string round the left and wind it back round itself (the right hand bit of string) at least three times, before pulling the left hand piece to tighten up, ready to pull the wood.

The Killick Hitch

Do one of these (above), before doing a timber hitch and a dragging we will go!

The quick release bowline – bowlines are loops that are easy to undo even when they have been put under a lot of strain.

 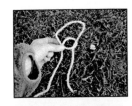 

Chapter 11

Community, Citizenship, Feasting and Celebrating

Being out in the woods at night, around a roaring fire awakens the tribal heart.

Every year the moon goes through a cycle of 13 full moons. This 13th chapter is the final chapter in the cycle of teachings the book offers. As mentioned at the outset of this learning journey, helping people to be native, to feel a part of their local ecological community has been one of the main aims of this book. I hope that by this stage in the journey cycle, you and your students do feel a little bit more native and 'of the land'. All that remains, then, is for us to tie up the loose ends and 'return the native' to the human community, with a game, something to build, some gifts, a feast and a celebration!

When we have been into the woods and return to our houses, villages, towns and cities, we bring a little natural magic, perhaps a sparkle in the eye, or a scent of wood smoke, back into the landscape dominated by the human. I like to think that nature takes a deep breath in, drawing us from our little boxes, into the heart of natural wonder, and then breathes us gently back out, to return to our own communities, spiritually refreshed.

It is my hope that through engaging with the activities in this book, people will feel the 'calling' from the wild places, a tug on the heartstrings that can only be fulfilled by going alone, somewhere wild and beautiful, perhaps camping out for a night or two, leaving nothing but footprints and gratitude, to return carrying some new wild vibe inside. I believe that this kind of experience enables a person to feel part of the natural order, to fully become a citizen of the planet, with something to offer one's own community.

Going into a wild place, to sleep in a simple shelter, by a fire we have lit, to eat some gathered food and collected water helps us feel more at home on the earth. It is a rite of passage. To venture deep into the wild, or in the woods, with ones fears and demons gathering like moths to a flame around a hearty campfire, can help us to feel at home in our bodies, to be more self assured, self confident and happy with our own company. From that place of personal bedrock, we can nurture our own garden of talents and share the surplus with our community, natural and human (if there is a difference).

One of the troubles of the modern world is a lack of community. Most people like to feel at though they are part of something - that they fit in, (especially teenagers, who naturally seem to flock together). But a gang is not really a community; a community needs people of all ages and various talents to keep it going. A community is based on communication, and it seems we have less and less of it in our western world, biased as it is towards transportation, and in spite of the advanced communications technology so widely available nowadays.

Community is at its best when its members are functioning for the common good. I believe it is part of our roles as environmental educators and mentors to encourage our pupils to give some of their energy into their communities. Here are some reasons why.

Ecological communities are more stable the more dynamic they are. Every organism gives something of him or herself and has a part to play. Gandhi, a great one for living by the principle of being the change you wish to see, advocated giving 10% of oness income to charity. Why 10%? It follows a natural pattern of energy accumulation in what are known in ecology as food pyramids. At the bottom of a pyramid are the producers, the plants. Of all the energy from the sun they use to grow and reproduce, 10% is available to the next layer in the pyramid, the herbivores. 10% of the energy these animals use to grow and reproduce is available to the carnivores, and so on. It's the reason there are very few 'top predators' in an ecosystem; there is only so much energy available.

It follows that at least 10% of an educational programme should be spent focussing on activities that build community, require teamwork, and work towards a common goal. Many of the activities I have described so far in the book are very suitable for developing teamwork: 'making blobster villages' and 'capture the flag', for example. Hopefully, some of the activities will have involved a bit of laughter too.

What follows are some more teambuilding activities, followed by a few personal suggestions and wider examples of simple community building.

The human woodlouse!
Group size: 4 or more (in multiple groups of 3-8)
Ages 7 and up
At least 15 minutes

Ready

This game involves a team of between 3 and 8 folk, being overseen by a guardian, feeling their way through a landscape towards a goal, another person beating a drum. It's great for developing empathy with animals because of the role-play element; by pretending to be a woodlouse (or centipede or caterpillar) we take a step towards getting under their exoskeleton and having more of an idea of what their lives may be like. This activity can be done with as few as four people – one person being the drumbeater and guardian, the rest making up the woodlouse. The person in front, the head of the woodlouse, is blindfolded and has feelers. The people being the body of the woodlouse are also blindfolded. As leader, ensure everyone gets a chance to be the 'head' at the front. You can choose to have short distances for the woodlouse to travel, changing the 'head' each time, or you can change the person being the 'head' every few minutes. Or you can do both, which is what I do most often.

You can also see if anyone else has ideas on other creatures you could mimic to continue the teamwork theme, or simply send the groups off to look for segmented minibeasts like woodlice and centipedes.

Get set

You will need blindfolds, feelers (thin, strong sticks about a metre long), drum or click-sticks, re-useable plastic cups, water, water-container.

Pick a few folks to be guardians – their role is to ensure the safety of the activity by going ahead of the woodlouse to scout for holes etc.

Choose an area to move through, gather your group and scratch out a start line. Someone is bound to ask, "What are you doing?"

Go!

"Who knows what a woodlouse looks like?" Keep questioning until you get the information that you want...that they have segmented bodies, loads of pairs of legs and a set of feelers coming out from the head, etc.

"I often wonder how all those legs manage to move, in such synchronicity, without all tangling up! It must really take some teamwork!"

"Who wants to play a game? It's called 'the woodlouse game'. In teams of up to 8, you will be given one pair of feelers (show the feelers and how to use them) and a blindfold for everyone. John, (our imaginary other leader), will go off over there, about 20-30 paces away, and bang a drum for you to home in on. He will start when we are all ready. Please get into teams, choose someone to be the head, and line up over here, in your centipede form, before putting your blindfolds on. I will give you the feelers when you are all ready. You will each get a go at being the head of the woodlouse."

Make sure there are a couple of metres between each woodlouse along the starting line.

"When you hear the drum start to beat, move with as much grace as possible towards the sound of the drum". John starts to drum, hitting the drum once every 10 seconds or more.

Thanks again to Chris Salisbury of Wildwise, for the last three pictures.

Have as many goes as it takes for everyone to have a turn at being the leader. Then, have one final go, in which the drumbeater walks ahead, about 15-30 yards in front, of the woodlice. When you, the leader, blow a whistle or make some kind of animal noise, each woodlouse team swaps its leader, without peeking, and then carries on, being overseen by their guardians of course!

When all the moving about is done, ask everyone to remove their blindfolds and then gather everyone in to find out what we can learn from this activity, such as:

- What qualities did you need to work well as a centipede?
- What makes a good leader?
- Who felt frustrated at times? Useless? Why?
- Who enjoyed it? Why?
- This activity isn't like football, when everyone is spread out on a field. What was it like being so close to your teammates?
- What do you think the blindfolds do to help the teamwork?.

The activity can be extended by; finding more difficult terrain to move through; changing the types of feelers; by the drummer moving away slowly; by giving the people being the body cups of water filled to the brim (to fill up a cooking pot be used for boiling the pasta later!). You can also see if anyone else has ideas on other creatures you could mimic to continue the teamwork theme, or simply send the groups off to go and look for segmented mini-beasts like woodlice and centipedes

Large Debris Shelter Building
Group size: 4-8 per shelter
Ages 8 and above
About 4 hours

Ready

Constructing something large with a communal function is another effective way of building community spirit. In days of old people helped build each other's houses and raised barns together. Building a 5-6 person shelter, with a central fire pit, is another way. The hearth, the central fire, is important as it is symbolic of the heart, and is the shared responsibility for the group's wellbeing. A communal shelter is more efficient with materials than solo shelters. Too big a shelter means the fire will be too far away from the beds, so 5-6 people is the optimum number for this activity

Get set

You will need an area with plenty of leaf litter and sticks. A surprisingly large amount of material is used to make a group shelter, though less of course, per person, than if you were to be making single person huts. An axe, folding saw, bushcraft knife and some string can be useful too, but not necessary, if your materials are suitable. You will need a couple of buckets for water to be kept inside the shelter.

Go!

Say there are 6 people who want to make a den to stay in for a few days. We choose a location where there is an abundance of materials, then join hands and form a circle and then all lie down head to toe, head to toe, along the perimeter of a circle, to see if the area is big enough. We then all gather three sticks (one person collects an extra set for the doorway):

- Two sticks with forks at the end, one as high as our waists, the other about as high as our armpits. These sticks can be sharpened at the other end to the fork to make the build a little easier.
- A straight beam, about wrist thick and a bit longer than we each are tall.

Lying down in a circle, we place the shorter of the two forked sticks on the ground to mark the place these uprights (the shorter forked sticks) need to be positioned. Stand up. Push the uprights into the ground just enough so they stand up unaided. The horizontal crossbeams go on next.

Now add the longer of the forked sticks to diagonally prop up the whole structure from the outside of the circle, where the beams and posts meet.

Then lay more and more straight sticks to cover the sleeping compartments, (which should each be big enough for the sleeper and his or her bags). Ideally, these should be positioned at an angle steeper than 45 degrees. It's good if these sticks are long enough to extend beyond the beams towards the fire – not too close, to give the sleeping areas more cover.

Thanks to Martin Prothero for these two photos.

Cover the sleeping areas with fine twigs and leaf litter or thatch. The covering will need to be at least a foot deep, preferably two, to keep the occupants dry on a rainy night.

These folks made their shelter as part of an OCN qualification in Woodland Survival Skills (the shelter is behind the smoke, top right, I know it is obscured, but I was the best picture I had, and the atmosphere of the picture is lovely)

When the house building has finished, and the builders settled in for a day or two youcould have a go at using knives and batons to make a totem pole, like these folks are doing.

The Give-away blanket

One of the loveliest ways of recycling and giving away precious things is to make a special give away blanket. Simply by laying out a blanket in a secluded place or specially created bower and then inviting people to leave special, but no longer needed items on the blanket for someone else to use encourages generosity, and letting go. The way I have done this has been to open up the give away blanket space for a fixed period of time, when people can come and part with their special things...(things like clothing, a necklace, Pokémon cards perhaps, and once I saw a didgeridoo being given away). When the give away time is 'closed', the blanket is then opened up for people to come if they wish, once person at a time, and choose a gift from the blanket.

A hunter-gatherer feast!

Feasting is one of the best ways to develop a community feeling! Pizzas cooked in a wood-fired oven can bring everybody together; there is wood to be collected, dough prepared, vet sliced, sauce made and cheese grated...

Del, Old Man of the Woods, serves up wood fired pizza!

Even something as simple as a shared picnic of packed lunches works in the same way. Another way is to have a hunter-gatherer feast, as outlined below.

189

Ready

Baked potatoes are relatively easy to cook in a campfire. How about meeting up with a group of friends, or going with your class, to a suitable wild place, and making a fire to bake potatoes in? Once the potatoes are in the fire, you can leave them, and go off in small groups to hunt and gather salad plants and greens to make a pesto, to go with the spuds. While the group is out foraging the fire keeper prepares chocolate bananas, and then hides them, for baking in the fire when the potatoes are done! You will need to start preparing about 2 hours before you want to feast.

Get set

You will need a spade, potatoes wrapped in tin foil for everybody (very bushcafty!) a just ripe banana for each person, and a large chocolate bar – enough for about 3 squares each. I would recommend taking thick leather gloves, plastic salad-collecting bowls, bowls for eating from, water to wash the salad in, grated cheese, butter or margarine, fire-making kit, cutlery, perhaps some scissors or a pestle and mortar to make the pesto, a clove of garlic, picnic blanket for laying out the salads on, baskets to carry everything in, balsamic vinegar, cold pressed olive oil and a donkey to carry it all for you!

Go!

As a group, we make a fire-pit, about a foot deep, and wide enough to pop all the potatoes in. We measure for this by laying all the potatoes out on the ground first, and marking out the area with a stick or the spade. We dig the pit, lining it with sand if there is any nearby, because it retains heat so well. We then build a big fire in the pit, with logs around the outside to form a box, and leave it to burn for a while. After about half an hour, the inner sides of the big logs should be burning well, not the outsides just yet. The rest of the wood should have just about burnt away. Without moving the big logs aside, (so your knees don't burn) push the potatoes into the ashes. Let the fire cook the potatoes slowly, perhaps by having thicker smouldering branches to burn over the top, resting between the logs round the edge. Too much fierce heat turns the potatoes into coal-like lumps.

We are now free to go off and forage! Taking a salad bowl between a few people, we collect wild herbs for the salad. It's a lovely thing to do in small groups, chatting as you pop a bit of this and a bit of that into the bowl. To make enough pesto for ten people you will need a carrier bag full of greens (young nettle tops, chickweed, cow parsley, wild pea greens and fennel is a favourite combination) chopped up really finely, or bashed with a pestle and mortar, mixed with a large, finely chopped clove of garlic, a generous pinch of grated cheese and a slosh of olive oil. Delicious. If you take about an hour foraging, then your spuds should be almost ready when you return. While the hunters are gathering, the fire keeper gets out the bananas, cut a slit along the top lip of the banana's smile and pops in a few pieces of chocolate.

Once the salads have been washed and some dressing made, it is time to get the potatoes out of the fire with the spade. Remove one of the logs from around the fire so that you can get the spade in, under the ashes and lift out the potatoes. Someone with a stick can tap the spade, while it is over the fire, to knock off some of the ashes. I lay the spade on the floor, holding it steady with one hand, and pick out the spuds with a gloved hand, laying them on rocks or leaves to stop them from getting dusty. Keeping the gloves on, peel off the tin foil and put it aside for recycling. The potatoes can then be cut open and given to the feasters to stuff full with butter, cheese, pesto and salad. Yum.

Then out come the bananas! Lay these on top of the embers, making sure they don't topple over, to bake until the chocolate has melted. They can be eaten, carefully, from the banana skin itself with practice, using a

spoon. Finish off with a round or two of jokes, or perhaps a story and singing around the fire.

Celebration – Leafy Firework displays!
All ages,
All group sizes,
At least 20 minutes, no more than an hour

Ready

In our multicultural world, there are thousands of good reasons for celebrating with fire, food, music, dance and song. Each morning we turn to face the sun. Birds sing. Every month there is a dark moon, a full moon, a new moon or another tree in the Celtic tree calendar. There are deity days for holy people from all the religions. There are periods of fasting, seasons of sowing, times for harvesting and feasts of loaves to celebrate new flour. We have rites of passage. There's Red Nose Day, Fridays, birthdays, and wakes. Almost all of them involve fire. Fire, and more recently fireworks, has been at the heart of human celebrations for millennia.

Seeing fire works one autumn inspired this activity. I was leading a play session in a park in Dursley. The autumn colours were especially vivid - yellows, reds and even purples. I started picking up leaves and sticks, and with a playful bunch of children from the local estate, made our own fireworks displays, by laying out patterns of leaves on the ground. It turned out to be a cunning way of looking at the symmetry of each of the leaves, and also in our displays. Some of the fireworks were amazing (black and white photos really don't cut the mustard I am afraid). We made up sound effects for each firework; a few little groups did actions too. Some of us ended up gathering armfuls of leaves, crouching down, and then jumping up releasing the leaves with a whiz-bang-pop! Go on... have a firework display of your own, because, whatever the occasion, it's a great way of celebrating! I finish with a jumping 'African clap'.

Get set

You will need an outdoor area, with access to sticks and leaves of many colours. Sweetie wrappers can be used too! Designate a place to lay out the displayed leaves.

Go!

Near the end of my time spent with a group I will say that we are soon going to have a little celebration to 'mark the end of our time together'. Whilst they are having a ten-minute break I prepare for it by making a leafy firework. I call my group over to have a look at it, do a silly and exaggerated firework noise and say, "Come on! Let's have a celebration and make our own massive firework display! You can work alone or in groups, and I want sound effects and actions as well!"

This was an amazing firework – deep purple, dark red and then bright yellow against the green of the grass worked really well.

When everybody is ready, we visit each leafy firework, watching and listening to the firework display as enacted by each participant. At each one we visit I get the whole group to repeat the firework display sound effect and action altogether! It's fun!

To finish the whole celebration I call everybody in, gather in a toe-to-toe circle for the final big bang. Once the circle is complete, we have a quick practice clap: "Right. To finish! The big bang! We need a quick practice. Let's all do one clap, altogether, like this, 1, 2, 3, clap! OK. Ready? 1,2,3,clap!"

Crouching down, beckoning everyone that can to follow suit, I then say,

"Thank you everybody for your fireworks, this is the last one. On the count of three let's jump up in the air and clap one big clap, altogether at the same time! When that is done the session is over, and it's time to go.

Ready? 1, 2, 3…!"

Suggested reading, resources and websites

The books are arranged into sections that seemed logical (to me!).
They are favourite books that have influenced, helped and inspired
me along the way. If there are any books (or websites) that you think I
should read, drop me a line to chris@wholeland.org.uk

Stories, Thinking and Art – some of the books that have
changed my worldview as a child, a university student, then parent
and educator.

George, Jean. *My Side of the Mountain,* London, Puffin, 2000

MacDonald, Margaret. *Earth Care: World folk tales to talk about,*
    North Have, CT, Linnet Books, 1999

Bates, Brian. *The Way of Wyrd*, London, Arrow Books, 1996

Capra, Fritjof. *The Web of Life: A New Synthesis of Mind and Matter*,
    London, HarperCollins 1996

Seed, John, et al. *Thinking like a Mountain. Towards a council of All
Beings.* London, Heretic Books, 1988

Gilbert, Ian. *Little Owl's Book of Thinking Skills*, Camarthen, Wales,
    Crown House Publishing 2004

Carter, Forrest. *The Education of Little Tree.* New Mexico University
    Press, 2001

Buhner, Stephen Harrod.   *The Lost language of Plants*, Vermont,
    Chelsea Green 2001

                The Secret Teachings of Plants,
    Rochester, VT, Bear and Company, 2004

Van Matre, Steve. *Earth Education,* Greenville, West Virginia, Institute
    of Earth Education, 1990

Cohen, Lawrence J. *Playful Parenting*, New York, Ballantine Books,
    2001

Goldsworthy, Andy. *Andy Goldworthy,* London, Penguin, 1990

Drury, Chris. *Found Moments in Time and Space*, New York,
Harry.N.Abrams 1998

Harding, Mike. *A little book of the Green Man.* Aurum Press LTD
England, 1998

Wild food, Herbal Medicine, Plants and Flowers -
these are the books I refer to most often.

Blamey, Marjorie, Richard Fitter and Alastair Fitter. *Wild Flowers of
    Britain and Ireland.* London, A&C Black Publishers 2003

Elpel, Thomas J. *Botany in a Day.* Pony, Montana, HOPS press, 2006

Podlech, Dieter. *Herbs and Healing Plants of Britain and Europe.*
    London, HarperCollins Publishers 1996

Bairacli Levy, Juliette de, *The Illustrated Herbal Handbook for Everyone*. London, Faber and Faber, 1974

Weise, Vivien. *Cooking Weeds*, Prospect Books, Totnes, 2004

Mabey, Richard. *Flora Britannica*. London, Chatto and Windus 1998

Messeuge, Maurice. *Of People and Plants*. Healing Arts Press, 1991

Duff, Gail. *The Countryside Cookbook*. Dorchester, Prism Press 1982

Bremness, Lesley. *The Complete Book of Herbs*. London, Dorling Kindersley 1990

Brown, Tom Jnr. *Tom Brown's Guide to Wild, Edible and Medicinal Plants*. New York, The Berkley Publishing Group 1985

Fern, Ken. *Plants for a Future*. Hampshire, UK Permanent Publications 1997

Mabey, Richard. *Food For Free*. London, HarperCollins Publishers 2001

Duffy, Kevin F. *Harvesting Nature's Bounty*. 2000

Burrows, Ian. *Food from the Wild*. London, New Holland Publishers 2005

Fearnley-Whittingstall, Hugh. *A Cook on the Wild Side*. London, Macmillan Publishers 1997

Phillips, Roger. *Wild Food*. London, Macmillan Publishers 1983

Homes and shelters from around the world

Kahn et al. *Shelter*, Shelter Publications inc, http://www:shelterpub.com USA, 1973 1990

Kahn, Lloyd. *HomeWork hand build shelter,* Bolinas, CA, 2004

Bushcraft, Survival and Wilderness Living Skills

Elpel, Thomas J. *Primitive Living, Self sufficiency and Survival,* Hops Press, Guilford, CT 2004

Davenport, Gregory. *Wilderness Living*. Pennsylvania, Stackpole Books 2001

Brown, Tom Jnr. *Tom Brown's Fieldguide to Wilderness Survival*. New York, The Berkley Publishing Group 1983

---------------- *Tom Brown's Fieldguide to Nature and Survival for Children*. New York, The Berkley Publishing Group 1989

Urquhart, Judy. *Living Off Nature*. Middlesex, Penguin Books 1980

Kochanski, Mors. *Bush Craft*. Renton USA, Lone Pine Publishing 1987

Mears, Raymond. *The Outdoor Survival Handbook*. New York, St Martin's Press 1992

Mears, Raymond. *Bushcraft*. London, Hodder and Stoughton 2002

Working with Wood and Mud

Mason, Bernard. *Woodcraft*. New York, A.S. Barnes and Company 1939

Tabor, Ray. *Green Woodworking Pattern Book*. London, Chrysalis Books 2005

Lubkemann, Chris. *Whittling*. East Petersburg, Fox Chapel Publishing 2005

Denzer, Kiko. *Dig Your Hands in the Dirt*, Blodgett, OR, USA, 2005

Trees

Jon Stokes et al. *Why are leaves green?* London, Tree Council, 2007

Miles, Archie. *Silva - The Tree In Britain*. London, Ebury Press 1999

Hageneder, Fred. *The Living Wisdom of Trees*. London, Duncan Baird Publishers 2005

Hageneder, Fred. *The Heritage of Trees*. Edinburgh, Floris Books 2001

Hageneder, Fred. *The Spirit of Trees*, Edinburgh, Floris Books 2000

Warren, Piers. *British Native Trees*. UK, Wildeye 2006

Paterson, Jacqueline Memory. *Tree Wisdom*. London, Thorsons 1996

Nature Awareness and Outdoor Play

Horsfall, Jacqueline. *Play Lightly on the Earth*. Nevada City, CA, Dawn Publications 1997

Cornell, Joseph. *Listening to Nature*. Nevada City, CA, Dawn Publications 1987

Cornell, Joseph *Sharing Nature With Children*. Nevada City, CA, Dawn Publications 1998

Cornell, Joseph *Sharing the Joy of Nature*. Nevada City, CA, Dawn Publications 1999

Young, Jon, Ellen Hass and Evan McGown. *Coyote's Guide to Connecting with Nature*. Shelton, WA, Owlink Media 2008

Masheder, Mildred. *Let's Enjoy Nature*. London, Green Print 1994

Masheder, Mildred. *Let's Play Together*. London, Green Print 1989

Ward, Jennifer. *I Love Dirt*. Boston, Shambala Publications 2008

Dyer, Alan and Hodgeson, John. *Let Your Children Go Back To Nature*. Somerset, Capall Bann Publishing 2003

Maclellan, Gordon. *Celebrating Nature*. Somerset, Capall Bann 2007

Caduto, Michael and Bruchac, Joseph. *Keepers of the Night*. Colerado, Fulcrum Publishing, 1994

Tracking and Field Guides – incredibly useful for finding out what some of the things are that busy eyes find. I also have a load of fold out charts that came with BBC Wildlife magazines one year, detailing things like Moths, Butterflies, Grasshoppers, pebbles, Trees, etc –the Wildlife trusts now do something similar, worth getting hold.

Brown, Roy et al. *Tracks and Signs of the Birds of Britain and Europe.* London, Christopher Helm 2003

Couzens, Dominic. *Birds by behaviour,* London, Collins, 2003

Bang & Dahlstrom. *Animal Tracks and Signs,* Oxford University Press, 2001

Evans, G. *The Observer's Book of Birds' Eggs*, London, Frederick Warne & Co LTD, 1965

Sterry, Paul. *Collins complete guide to British Wildlife*, London, HarperCollins Publishing 1997

Rezendez, Paul. *Tracking and the art of seeing.* Collins 1999

Festivals and celebrations

Kindred, Glennie. *Sacred Celebrations*, Gothic Image Publications, Glastonbury, 2001

Carey and Large. *Festivals, Families and Food*, Stroud, Hawthorne Press, 1982

Maclellan, Gordon. *Celebrating Nature.* Somerset, Capall Bann 2007

Audio and websites

Jon Young has produced a truly amazing set of audio learning material, worth every cent, available on tape and CD from http//www.OWLinkmedia.com: Seeing Through Native Eyes, Tracking Pack One, Advanced Bird Language and The Art of Mentoring.

Things we use fire for:

Cooking, roasting, boiling, melting, grilling, heating, lighting, signaling, combustion engines, making electricity, hardening wood, steam bending wood, cauterizing, smelting metal, working metal, firing pottery, ceremonies and celebrations, offerings, smoking hides, preserving food, making charcoal, making gunpowder, bombs, keeping insects away with smoke, keeping predators away, fighting with, performance and last but certainly not least, company.

About Chris Holland and Wholeland

Guided by the principle of "**learn to play, play to learn**", Chris Holland provides light hearted, yet serious, whole body learning, training and teambuilding experiences to help people reconnect with the land and all our relations. Chris has many things in his teaching bundle. He is a bushcraft teacher, an outdoor play and nature awareness facilitator, an environmental artist, musician and storyteller who delivers events  workshops, training, teambuilding and parties. He is also beginning to run I love my World camps, see www.ilovemyworldcamps.co.uk for more details from spring 2010

Chris was born in Sussex in the early 70's, taken to Australia by his dad a few years later, only to go to Kenya with his mum when he was seven. He played a lot outdoors, struggled on at a number of different schools in a number of different countries, felt very chuffed when he received an Honours degree in Environmental Science, and has been teaching, instructing and mentoring in and out of schools since 1993. He is finding ways of educating youngsters in bushcraft and nature awareness through the national curriculum in schools, through play, through Forest School and by stealth! He likes teaching older folks too of course. He leads 'expotitions' along the River Otter and onto Dartmoor. He works with **Wildwise** Environmental Education and Training, and was the Earthwise Education Ranger at Otterton Mill.

Wholeland was established in 2000 by Chris Holland to bring people, young and old, into a more meaningful, loving, respectful, joyous and spirited relationship with the earth, plants and animals from which the majority of our resources come, in the hope that this will help humans want to live in a more balanced and sustainable way. Chris has many things in his teaching bundle. He is a bushcraft teacher, an outdoor play and nature awareness facilitator, an environmental artist, musician and storyteller who runs training, teambuilding and parties too. Wholeland is based in Otterton, East Devon.

Call Chris on 07980 601830, or visit www.wholeland.org.uk

PS, Have fun out there!

LaVergne, TN USA
22 February 2011

217449LV00001B/312/P